Anne M. Holehan.

570·7

BIOMETRICAL
INTERPRETATION

NEIL
GILBERT

INSTITUTE OF
ANIMAL ECOLOGY,
UNIVERSITY OF
BRITISH COLUMBIA

Biometrical
Interpretation

94,113

CLARENDON PRESS

OXFORD

1973

Oxford University Press, Ely House, London W. 1

GLASGOW   NEW YORK   TORONTO   MELBOURNE   WELLINGTON
CAPE TOWN   IBADAN   NAIROBI   DAR ES SALAAM   LUSAKA   ADDIS ABABA
DELHI   BOMBAY   CALCUTTA   MADRAS   KARACHI   LAHORE   DACCA
KUALA LUMPUR   SINGAPORE   HONG KONG   TOKYO

© OXFORD UNIVERSITY PRESS 1973

4231

Text set in 10/12pt. IBM Press Roman, printed by photolithography,
and bound in Great Britain at The Pitman Press, Bath

'If your experiment needs statistics, you ought to have done a better experiment . . .'

Lord Rutherford

PREFACE

THIS book is addressed to biologists who use biometrical methods as a tool. It is not the usual book of statistical recipes. These days, we have computers to do the 'donkey work': so the biologist need not know how to calculate, say, a regression coefficient. But he does need, more than ever, to understand the use and interpretation of regressions. This book concentrates not on how to do an analysis, but on how to choose the right sort of analysis, and on how to make sense of the answer. It deals with questions that often arise in practice. So it is written in self-defence, to answer questions which biologists ask again and again.

The first three chapters deal with basic statistical methods. Some parts are unavoidably complex. If you can cope with those three chapters (and with their examples), you have nothing to fear from statistics. The going is easier in later chapters. Chapters 10 and 11 are about two fields of biology which rely heavily on mathematics and statistics.

R. A. Fisher once defined variance as 'the attitude of one statistician to another'. We can look at any particular question from several points of view. Statistical methods, apparently quite unrelated to each other, are in fact different aspects of the same central theory. Not everyone will agree with my point of view, which is roughly that of the Rothamsted school; Chapters 7 and 10 in particular, which are specialized ones, will, very possibly, enrage some of the experts.

The book assumes some familiarity with elementary statistical methods. For further reading, I recommend Bailey (1959). Technical questions are lucidly explained by Kendall and Stuart (1963). The examples in this book are often fictitious, but employ real data drawn from other sources. They should preferably be done by computer, where possible. I thank several colleagues in Australia, Britain and Canada for their criticisms, and the many students who acted as guinea-pigs.

Vancouver, 1972   N.E.G.

CONTENTS

Contents

1 | LEAST SQUARES

STATISTICAL methods are used to *describe* sets of data, and to *predict* (as well as possible) the values of other measurements which have not, or cannot, be made. The emphasis is on prediction. Nearly always, a set of data is only a sample; we are interested, not just in that particular sample, but in the whole population from which the sample is drawn. For example, we may have measurements on twenty Dalmatian dogs, but we wish to draw conclusions about Dalmatians, or perhaps even dogs, in general. This means that we wish to make predictions, from the sample of twenty, about other animals which we have not seen, and may never see. We cannot expect those predictions to be perfectly accurate, but we want them to be as good as possible.

Suppose that we are interested in some measurement y. The value of y, measured on the ith dog, is y_i. We are going to divide the value y_i into two parts, F_i and a remainder. For F_i we choose some function whose value we can supply, and which will help us predict future values of y_i. Very often, F_i is a mean, the same for all dogs. Or F_i might represent a mean for male dogs and a mean for bitches, in which case we cannot supply its value in any given case until we know the sex of the animal concerned. Or F_i might be a regression of y_i on some other measurement x_i, so that we need to know x_i before we can supply F_i for any given animal. The basic principle is the same:

$$y_i = F_i + \text{remainder},$$

where F_i is a value which we can supply in any particular case, and which helps us to predict y_i; while the 'remainder', or 'residual', means 'a bit left over which we cannot, or cannot be bothered to, specify'. The same distinction between what we know (F_i) and what we do not know (remainder) occurs in the closely related subjects of statistical mechanics and information theory. The remainder arises in two ways. It may be an error of measurement: we can never measure anything exactly, although we can *count* exactly. Or the remainder may represent something biological, which we cannot, or cannot be bothered to, predict. For example, the measurement y might be the number of eggs in a clutch of duck eggs. We may be content to say that a duck lays, on average, 4·6 eggs. Then $F_i = 4·6$ in every case, but no duck can lay exactly 4·6 eggs. If a duck actually lays five eggs, the residual is +0·4. We know that there are physiological processes which decide that a particular duck shall lay 1, 2, 3, 4 . . eggs, but we cannot specify — or perhaps we are not interested in — the precise number for any given duck. The word 'error' is often used instead of 'remainder'. But the word error implies some kind of mistake; it suggests that the duck ought to lay 4·6 eggs. The terminology has, in the past, trapped some biologists into regarding genuine biological variation as a regrettable nuisance. I shall reserve the term 'error' for errors of measurement. The words 'remainder' and 'residual' mean the same thing, and will be used interchangeably.

The value of F_i may sometimes be supplied theoretically, but usually it is estimated from a sample of data. In that case, we want the estimate to give the best possible predictions, i.e. to make the residuals as small as possible. It is up to us to specify what *kind* (mean, regression, etc.) of function F_i should be; it is unfortunate if we choose an F_i which is incapable of predicting y_i. For example, we might suppose that some average m can predict future values of y. (I shall make the usual distinction between the unknown population mean m, and its known estimate $\bar{y}$.) Then we shall have

$$y_i = m + \text{remainder},$$

and we want the estimate of m to make the remainders, in the whole population, as small as possible. We therefore use an estimate of m which makes the remainders in the observed sample small. Very often, we estimate m by minimizing $\Sigma(y_i - m)^2$ — that is, the sum of squares of all the remainders in the sample. We might, instead, estimate m by minimizing some other combination of the sample remainders $(y_i - m)$. However, the sum of squares offers many advantages. It leads to simple methods of calculation. It puts positive and negative remainders on an equal footing, and pays greater attention to large remainders than to small: for example, a remainder of −1 contributes 1 to the sum of squares, while a remainder of +2 contributes 4. There are also theoretical reasons (mentioned in Chapter 7) for preferring the sum of squares. It can be shown that the estimate of m which minimizes $\Sigma(y_i - m)^2$ is the arithmetic mean $\bar{y}$ of the sample values of y. We use the fact that $\bar{y}$ minimizes the sum of squares of the remainders, to *justify* our use of the arithmetic mean $\bar{y}$, rather than any other combination of the values of y. Similarly, if we suppose that y can be predicted by a linear regression on some known measurement x, so that $F_i = a + bx_i$, the customary estimates of a and b are those that minimize $\Sigma(y_i - a - bx_i)^2$, summed over all values of y_i (with concomitant x_i) in the sample.

If the sample values of y are 31, 32, 29, 31, 30, 28, 30, and 29, it is reasonable to suppose that future values of y will also be somewhere near the sample mean 30·0, so that the equation, $y = 30·0 + $ residual, is likely to predict values of y better than the equation $y = 0 + $ residual. In other words, the sample mean is significantly different from zero. But if the values of y are 1, 2, −1, 1, and 0, it is doubtful if the sample mean gives a worthwhile prediction of other values of y. The mean is not significantly different from zero, and it does not pay, on the evidence of these data alone, to think in terms of a non-zero mean m. You may say, 'Cannot a mean of zero predict y just as well as a mean of 30?' It cannot. A mean of zero can *describe* the ys all right (Chapter 2 will examine the descriptive use of means), but to say 'I expect that $y = 0 + $ an unpredictable remainder' is just the same as saying, 'I expect that $y = $ something unpredictable'. So long as the emphasis is on prediction, a zero mean does not help.

We not only use the sample values of y to estimate m, but we also use them to assess whether that estimate will indeed help us predict other values of y. The significance test tries to determine whether the remainder $(y_i - \bar{y})$ will usually be smaller than y_i itself. If so, $\bar{y}$ gives useful prediction of y_i. Since $\bar{y}$ is estimated by minimizing $\Sigma(y_i - m)^2$, the question is whether $\Sigma(y_i - \bar{y})^2$ is much less than the original sum of squares, Σy_i^2. Unless $\bar{y}$ chances to be exactly zero, $\Sigma(y_i - \bar{y})^2$ will necessarily come out less than Σy_i^2, since $\bar{y}$ is estimated by minimizing the sum of squares. So we ask, How much smaller must $\Sigma(y_i - \bar{y})^2$ be for $\bar{y}$ to be significant? To answer that question we do not consider the sum of squares itself. It is here that the ideas of 'degrees of freedom' and 'mean square' arise. Whereas m is estimated by minimizing the sum of squares, we use the *mean* square to assess whether the estimation has been worthwhile. The expression 'mean square of y' means just that — it is a mean value of y^2. Suppose we draw a sample of N values of y from a population with mean zero and variance V. The variance is defined as the average value, in the population as a whole, of $(y_i - m)^2$: so, in this case, when $m = 0$, the average value of y_i^2 is V. Then it can be shown (Example 8, Chapter 2) that the value of Σy_i^2 in the sample will,

3

on average, be NV, and that of $\Sigma(y_i - \bar{y})^2$ will, on average, be $(N - 1)V$. If we say that Σy_i^2 has N degrees of freedom and $\Sigma(y_i - \bar{y})^2$ has $(N - 1)$ degrees of freedom, then the mean squares $\Sigma y_i^2/N$ and $\Sigma(y_i - \bar{y})^2/(N - 1)$ are both expected to equal V, provided that the population mean m is zero. In other words, if $\bar{y}$ cannot predict values of y at all (because m is zero), we expect the 'remainder' mean square $\Sigma(y_i - \bar{y})^2/(N - 1)$ to equal the original mean square $\Sigma y_i^2/N$, but, if the 'remainder' mean square is smaller than the original mean square, *either* it is smaller by chance *or* $\bar{y}$ (the estimate of m) can usefully predict values of y.

We may look at the same matter from a slightly different point of view. If we doubled the size N of the sample, we should expect to get a sum of squares approximately twice as big. But there would be approximately twice as many degrees of freedom, and so, on average, the mean square would be the same. The original mean square $\Sigma y_i^2/N$ estimates the average value of y^2 or, in other words, of $(m + \text{remainder})^2$. The 'remainder' mean square $\Sigma(y_i - \bar{y})^2/(N - 1)$ estimates the remainder variance, i.e. the average value of $(\text{remainder})^2$. Therefore, if m is not zero, we expect the 'remainder' mean square to be less than the original mean square. We use a significance test to assess whether the reduction in the 'remainder' mean square can reasonably be attributed to chance. If not, we may use $\bar{y}$ to predict future values of y with some confidence.

For technical reasons, the variance-ratio (or F-) test does not directly compare the original and 'remainder' mean squares. Instead, it compares the size of the *reduction* in variance, achieved by fitting $\bar{y}$, with the size of the 'remainder' mean square (by 'fitting $\bar{y}$' we mean the whole process of calculating $\bar{y}$ and using it to calculate the residuals). The two comparisons are equivalent. The analysis of variance splits the original sum of squares into two parts: (1) the 'remainder' sum of squares, and (2) the difference, accounted for by the fitting of $\bar{y}$, between the original and 'remainder' sums of squares. These two parts of the original total sum of squares correspond exactly to the two parts (remainder and F_i) of y_i. Both parts of the sum of squares are then converted to mean squares by dividing each by its appropriate degrees of freedom – in this case, the 'remainder' sum of squares by $(N - 1)$ and the 'sum of squares due to fitting the mean' by 1. If the population mean is zero, these two mean squares are expected to be equal, since they both estimate a purely residual variance. (You may object that, if m is zero, it cannot account for any of the variance, i.e. the sum of squares due to fitting the mean ought to be zero. However, we can never know m exactly: we have to fit the sample mean $\bar{y}$ instead, and $\bar{y}$, in general, will not be zero, even when the population mean $m = 0$. As mentioned above, the fitting of $\bar{y}$ always produces *some* reduction in the 'residual' sum of squares, except in the rare case when $\bar{y}$ chances to be precisely zero.) The variance-ratio test then compares the 'mean square due to fitting the mean' with the 'remainder' mean square. But the essential question is, Does $\bar{y}$ give a worthwhile reduction in the remainder mean square? We must always remember that, however well some F_i may predict values of y_i, the important thing (statistically) is the 'remainder' mean square, which measures how much we do not know about y_i. Statements like 'the regression accounts for 86 per cent of the original variance' really mean 'the regression fails to account for 14 per cent of the variance'.

We may try this analysis on the data given above. The mean of the eight values 31, 32, 29, 31, 30, 28, 30, and 29 is 30·0. The residuals are therefore 1, 2, −1, 1, 0, −2, 0, and −1. The sum of squares of the original values is 7212, the sum of squares of the remainders is 12 and so the analysis of variance is:

	Degrees of freedom	Sum of squares	Mean square
due to fitting the mean	1	7200	7200·00
residual	7	12	1·71
total original	8	7212	901·50.

Fitting the mean therefore reduces the mean square from 901·50 to 1·71. The corresponding variance ratio is 7200·00/1·71. Very often, as in this case, the over-all mean is so obviously different from zero, that we automatically fit the mean as a preliminary step, before the analysis proper begins. In that case, the 'sum of squares due to fitting the mean' is called the 'correction for the mean', and we start the analysis with $N - 1$ degrees of freedom. But there is no need to subtract the 'correction for the mean' in those cases where $\bar{y}$ does not differ significantly from zero; and, occasionally, it is not necessary to fit a mean, even though $\bar{y}$ obviously differs from zero. We shall meet such a case in Chapter 3, namely, a regression which must go through the origin.

The worked example shows why the variance ratio does not directly compare the original and 'remainder' mean squares. The original sum of squares (7212) *includes* the 'remainder' sum of squares (12). So the 'remainder' mean square (1·71) is in some sense part of the original mean square (901·5); whereas 7200·00, the mean square due to fitting

Least Squares

the mean, and 1·71, the 'remainder' mean square, are distinct, independent entities. The variance-ratio test can only compare two mean squares which are independent; neither sum of squares may 'contain' the other sum of squares, or any part of it. If the variance ratio is calculated to be less than one, it means that the original mean square was actually rather smaller than the 'residual' mean square, so that the analysis has certainly not achieved a worthwhile reduction in the mean square. That is the reason why published tables of variance ratio only consider values greater than one.

Very often, then, the over-all mean obviously differs significantly from zero, and we are more interested in the difference between the means of two or more blocks of data. In that case, there is no doubt that fitting an over-all mean greatly reduces the size of the 'residual' mean square, and we want to know if a *further* reduction may be made by fitting separate means for each block. For example, is there any point in treating males and females separately? (There is, clearly, no sense in asking that question, unless we can allocate each individual to its appropriate category, in this case male and female.) Suppose that the values of y for males are 31, 32, 29, 31, 30 and those for females 28, 30, 29. Fitting the over-all mean will evidently give precisely the same analysis as before. The separate means for males and females are 30·6 and 29·0. The male residuals are therefore 0·4, 1·4, −1·6, 0·4, and −0·6, and the female residuals are −1·0, 1·0, and 0. The sum of the squares of all these residuals is 7·20. So, by fitting separate means for males and females, we get an analysis of variance:

	Degrees of freedom	Sum of Squares	Mean square
due to fitting male and female means	2	7204·80	3602·40
remainder	6	7·20	1·20
original	8	7212·00	901·50

The first line may be split:

	Degrees of freedom	Sum of squares	Mean square
fitting over-all mean (as before)	1	7200·00	7200·00
extra for separate male, female	1	4·80	4·80
remainder	6	7·20	1·20
original	8	7212·00	901·50

If we automatically correct for the over-all mean before we start the analysis, we get the usual analysis of variance:

	Degrees of freedom	Sum of squares	Mean square
males versus females, i.e. 'between sexes'	1	4·80	4·80
remainder, i.e. 'within sexes'	6	7·20	1·20
total (corrected for mean)	7	12·00	1·71

By distinguishing males from females, we reduce the 'residual' mean square from 1·71 to 1·20. The variance ratio 4·80/1·20 is not significantly large, indicating that the reduction from 1·71 to 1·20 may well be fortuitous. Although the values of y may possibly be smaller, on average, for females than for males, the existing sample does not furnish enough evidence to make the distinction worthwhile. If the male and female sample means were identical, both would equal the over-all sample mean, and so there would be *no* extra reduction in the 'residual' sum of squares. Therefore, the mean square labelled 'males versus females' is indeed concerned with the average difference *between* males and females (see Example 1(b), Chapter 6). Equally, the 'remainder' sum of squares is made up of terms $(y_i - \bar{y})^2$, where y_i is a male (or female) observation, and $\bar{y}$ is the corresponding male (female) mean. So the 'remainder' sum of squares is made up from differences between male and males, or between female and females, i.e. from differences *within* the set of males, and *within* the set of females. It is not affected by (i.e. it is independent of) the average difference between males and females. The whole analytic process of trying to reduce the 'residual' mean square may be continued step-by-step, to see if any more detailed categorization improves the prediction of values of y.

So far, we have implicitly assumed that all the values of y were measured with equal accuracy: each y has been given the same weight in the sum of squares. But sometimes we have to recognize that different ys have different accuracies; we then wish to pay more attention to the more accurate values. Instead of a sum of squares $\Sigma(y_i - F_i)^2$, we use a weighted sum of squares $\Sigma w_i(y_i - F_i)^2$. Here, w_i is the weight given to y_i. The usual, unweighted sum of squares is a special case of the weighted sum of squares, when every $w_i = 1$. If F_i represents an over-all mean m, the least-squares estimate of m (i.e. the

Least Squares

estimate of m which minimizes the weighted sum of squares) is the weighted sample mean $\bar{y} = \Sigma w_i y_i / \Sigma w_i$. If every $w_i = 1$, this reduces to the usual unweighted expression $\bar{y} = \Sigma y_i / N$. If we use a weighted mean, we must also use a weighted analysis of variance, that is, an analysis of the weighted sums of squares. This shows how intimately the estimate $\bar{y}$ is related to the analysis of variance. The unweighted mean does not minimize the weighted sum of squares, nor does the weighted mean minimize the unweighted sum of squares. To use a weighted mean in an unweighted analysis of variance (or vice versa) would be misleading, and therefore wrong.

Suppose that the variance V_i of the errors of measurement is not the same for every y_i in the sample. The most accurate value of $\bar{y}$ (i.e. that with the least error variance) is obtained by using a weight w_i equal to $1/V_i$. That means that an inaccurate value of y, with a large variance, is given a small weight. The weighted sum of squares then becomes $\Sigma(y_i - F_i)^2 / V_i$. When dealing with continuous measurements (e.g. lengths or temperatures) we usually do not need to weight the analysis, because we can reasonably assume that V_i does not vary very much, in which case the weighted and unweighted analyses will return much the same biological answer. The point is discussed further in Chapter 5. Now suppose that y_i is a count which can take only discrete values 0, 1, 2 . . . , and suppose that the expected value of y_i and F_i; the Poisson distribution tells us to expect that V_i will equal the mean F_i. The weighted sum of squares then becomes $\Sigma(y_i - F_i)^2 / F_i$, which is the usual expression for χ^2 (chi-squared) used in the analysis of data which take the form of counts. So the χ^2 analysis is a special case of the analysis of weighted sums of squares.

When we have to do a perplexing statistical analysis, we can always, in theory, return to first principles and minimize the appropriate sum of squares (or maximize the appropriate likelihood − Chapter 7). But, in a complicated case, the process of minimization may be just as perplexing. In practice, therefore, we work at a more superficial level, but using rules of statistical manipulation which are founded on least squares (or likelihood). These rules are examined in Chapters 2 and 3.

Examples 1

(1) The sample values of y are 31, 32, 29, 31, 30, 28, 30, and 29. Calculate $\Sigma(y - m)^2$ for $m = 0, 10, 20, 30, 40$, and 50. Plot the values of $\Sigma(y - m)^2$ against m, to show that $\Sigma(y - m)^2$ is minimized when m = the sample mean (30). Using the plot, show how Σy^2, i.e.

$\Sigma(y - 0)^2$, is split into $\Sigma(y - \bar{y})^2$ plus a part accounted for by fitting $\bar{y}$. Is there a value of m which reduces $\Sigma(y - m)^2$ to zero?

The next two examples require elementary algebra or calculus. They illustrate Chapter 1, but are not essential.

(2) Show that, for *any* set of ys, $\Sigma(y - m)^2$ is minimized when $m = \bar{y}$.

(3) Show that in a sample of N values of y with mean $\bar{y} = \Sigma y / N$,

$$\Sigma(y - \bar{y})^2 = \Sigma y^2 - N\bar{y}^2,$$

and, hence, that

Σy^2	$=$	$\Sigma(y - \bar{y})^2$	$+$	$(\Sigma y)^2 / N$
original sum of squares		remainder sum of squares		sum of squares due to fitting the mean

Verify this equation using the data of Example 1.

(4) The term 'degrees of freedom' is perplexing. It is often used, as in this chapter, to mean 'the divisor needed to convert a sum of squares into a mean square which will estimate the population variance V'. For example, Σy_i^2 has N degrees of freedom, and $\Sigma(y_i - \bar{y})^2$ has $N - 1$ degrees of freedom, because $\Sigma y_i^2 / N$ will, on average, equal V, if the population mean m is zero; and so will $\Sigma(y_i - \bar{y})^2 / (N - 1)$, whatever the value of m. The name 'degrees of freedom' arises in the following way. Once the value of $\bar{y}$ has been fixed, we could choose any values we liked for $N - 1$ of the y_is, but then the remaining value of y would have to follow automatically, in order to give the right value of the sample mean $\bar{y}$. More precisely, the N values of $(y_i - \bar{y})$ must sum to zero, and so only $N - 1$ of them are free to vary independently. Once $\bar{y}$ is fixed, the remainders $(y_i - \bar{y})$ have $N - 1$ 'degrees of freedom'. It can be shown theoretically (e.g. Example 8, Chapter 2) that the 'degrees of freedom' is indeed the right divisor to use, to estimate V (but see Example 3, Chapter 4).

2 | MEANS AND VARIANCES

CHAPTER 1 showed how we use means to predict values of y, i.e. to reduce the size of the 'remainder'. In this chapter, the means will be treated as entities in their own right. The chapter is full of formulae, but the only difficult part is about two-way tables.

A single mean can describe and summarize a whole set of values of y. Its actual size will answer practical questions by telling us 'how much'. For example, given an average yield of wheat, we can decide how many acres to grow. Significance and practical importance are not the same thing. It can happen that, although two means are significantly different, the difference is too small to bother about in practice. For instance, a new variety of wheat may consistently outyield an existing variety by 1 per cent; but that extra yield may not cover the cost of multiplying-up seed stocks, and releasing the new variety on the market. Although a mean is really a predictor of individual values of y, we may also regard it as a descriptive 'statistic' in its own right.

One mean cannot entirely summarize a set of data. The two distributions shown in Fig. 2.1 are evidently quite different, although both have a mean of 30. To describe a distribution, we need to quote both its mean and its variance — or, equivalently, its standard deviation. (If the distribution has some further peculiarity, e.g. if it is skew, still

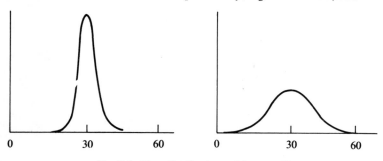

Fig. 2.1. Two distributions with mean 30.

further description may be needed.) This takes us into the world of variances, standard deviations, and standard errors. It is very important to grasp the elementary rules for handling these various quantities, otherwise, you will be left floundering in a mire of Ns, $(N-1)$s, and square roots. The rules are given in every textbook, but we shall re-examine them here.

Suppose we wish to *describe* the distribution of y from a sample of N values. The average value $\bar{y}$ is $\Sigma y/N$. It is sometimes called a measure of location, because it locates the whereabouts of the values of y on the scale of measurement. We must also quote some measure of the spread, or dispersion, which will distinguish between the two cases in Fig. 2.1. In other words, we want some measure of the absolute size of $y_i - \bar{y}$. Following the ideas of Chapter 1, we turn to the sum of squares $\Sigma(y_i - \bar{y})^2$. The sum of squares will not do as it stands, because we know that, as the sample size N increases, so does the sum of squares. However, the mean square $\Sigma(y_i - \bar{y})^2/(N-1)$ remains approximately constant. It estimates the variance of single values of y. Thus the sample mean $\bar{y}$ estimates the over-all average m of the whole population of values of y; and the sample mean square s^2 estimates the average of $(y-m)^2$, i.e. the variance V of individual values of y. So, the mean square *estimates* V, just as $\bar{y}$ *estimates* m. The square root of the sample mean square is called the standard deviation, or root mean square. It is a measure of the average deviation of y from the population mean m. The mean, mean square, and standard deviation are all concerned with individual values of y in the original population. They are, on average, unaffected by any change in sample size.

Usually, our sample of ys is a small sample from a large population. So the sample mean $\bar{y}$ is an inaccurate estimate of the population mean m. The bigger the sample size, the smaller the inaccuracy. We use a 'standard error' to estimate the size of that inaccuracy. The standard error is not concerned with the original population, but with the sample mean $\bar{y}$. So the standard error indicates the accuracy of the *sample mean*, and the standard deviation measures the variability of the individual values in the *population*. Unfortunately, the word 'variance' is used in both these connections; we talk about 'the variance of a population' and 'the variance of a mean'. If s^2 is the value of the 'residual' mean square — i.e. s^2 is an estimate of the population variance V — we estimate the variance of $\bar{y}$ as s^2/N. (This assumes that the residuals of successive values of y are uncorrelated, i.e. that there is no tendency for one residual to be specially large, just because some other residual turns out large.) 'The variance of $\bar{y}$' is defined as the average value of $(\bar{y} - m)^2$ which we should obtain if we took a whole set of different samples, each of size N, and worked out a $\bar{y}$ for each sample. The standard error of $\bar{y}$ is the square root of the variance of $\bar{y}$, i.e. it is $\sqrt{(s^2/N)}$. It is a measure of the average deviation of $\bar{y}$ from m. If we doubled the sample size N, the 'residual' mean square s^2 (i.e. the estimate of the variance of single y-observations) would remain approximately the same; but the estimated variance of $\bar{y}$, which is s^2/N, would be approximately halved, and so the standard error of $\bar{y}$ would be reduced by a factor $\sqrt{2}$. This means that, to double the accuracy of $\bar{y}$, we must multiply the sample size by 4; but to improve the accuracy of $\bar{y}$ tenfold, we must multiply N by 100.

There are two ways of joining the last two paragraphs together. Firstly, a single value of y might be regarded as a sample of size $N = 1$. Thus the standard deviation (which refers to any one original observation) is the standard error of a single value of y (regarding that value as an estimate of the population mean m). Secondly, we divide the corrected sum of squares $\Sigma(y_i - \bar{y})^2$ by the degrees of freedom $(N - 1)$ to get s^2, the 'remainder' mean square. The value of s^2 will come out much the same, however large the sample size N. To estimate the variance of the sample mean $\bar{y}$, we further divide s^2 by N, because $\bar{y}$ is the mean of N values of y. This variance of $\bar{y}$ (i.e. s^2/N) decreases as N increases, because $\bar{y}$ becomes more accurate as the sample gets bigger. So, in a formula like 'the variance of $\bar{y}$ is $\Sigma(y_i - \bar{y})^2/N(N - 1)$', the N and $N - 1$ are serving quite different purposes. The $N - 1$ is the degrees of freedom, needed to reduce the sum of squares to a mean square which estimates the variance of single values of y, and the N is there because $\bar{y}$ is the mean of N different values of y.

There are some simple rules for manipulating means and variances. If the variance of y is V and a is a constant, the variance of ay is a^2V. If the variance of y_1 is V_1 and the variance of y_2 is V_2, the variance of $y_1 + y_2$ is $V_1 + V_2$, provided that y_1 and y_2 are uncorrelated. These rules hold true whatever the ys may be (original observations, means, totals, or regression coefficients). We may combine the two rules by saying that the variance of $a_1y_1 + a_2y_2 + \ldots$ is $a_1^2 V_1 + a_2^2 V_2 + \ldots$, provided that the ys are uncorrelated. This formula may be used to work out any particular case that may arise. For example, if we put $a_1 = 1$ and $a_2 = -1$, the variance of $y_1 - y_2$ is $V_1 + V_2$, which is also the variance of $y_1 + y_2$. To get the variance of the sum, or of the difference, of two numbers, we add together their respective variances. We can use the same rule to find the variance of a mean. If we have N different ys, and if we put $a_1, a_2 \ldots a_N$ all equal to $1/N$. we find the variance of $\bar{y}$ (i.e. the variance of $y_1/N + y_2/N + \ldots + y_N/N$) is $V_1/N^2 + V_2/N^2 + \ldots V_N/N^2$. If the Vs are all the same, the variance of $\bar{y}$ is therefore NV/N^2, or V/N. So, the variance of the mean is $1/N$ times the variance of a single observation, as stated before. The condition that the ys shall be uncorrelated is very important.† If the ys are correlated, extra terms (called 'covariances') must accordingly be added to the formula. When we use the formula in practice, the estimates of V are usually calculated from *'remainder'* mean squares, and it is the *remainders* which have to be uncorrelated; this is usually the case, since the original ys have been measured independently from independent biological materials (e.g. different animals). There are also rules for finding the variance of $y_1 \times y_2$, of y^2, of y_1/y_2, or of any other non-additive combination of ys, but it is best to seek expert advice when such problems arise.

Suppose that we wish to compare two means $\bar{y}_1$ and $\bar{y}_2$. The variance of $\bar{y}_1 - \bar{y}_2$ is $V_1 + V_2$, provided that the $\bar{y}$s are uncorrelated, and so it is the *variances* that add together, not the standard errors. We have already met this additive property of variances in another guise in Chapter 1, where we divided the total sum of squares into a part accounted for by the mean plus a remainder part. Because of their additive properties, we work primarily with variances. For example, if $\bar{y}_1$ has standard error s_1 and $\bar{y}_2$ has standard error s_2, the variance of $\bar{y}_1 - 2\bar{y}_2$ is $s_1^2 + 4s_2^2$, i.e. we work in terms of the variances s_1^2 and s_2^2. Only at the very end of the calculation do we find the standard error, in this case $\sqrt{(s_1^2 + 4s_2^2)}$, by taking the square root of the variance.

In the example considered in Chapter 1, the 'residual' mean square (after fitting the means for male and female) is $1 \cdot 20$. This is an estimate of the variance of individual measurements, applying equally to males and females. (If we had suspected that males and females had different variances, we should, accordingly, have estimated those variances separately.) The mean for males is $30 \cdot 6$, and since it is the mean of five observations, its variance is estimated as $1 \cdot 20/5$. Similarly, the variance of the female mean ($29 \cdot 0$) is $1 \cdot 20/3$. The difference between the means

†The rule for finding the variance of $a_1 y_1 + a_2 y_2 + \ldots$ works only if the ys are uncorrelated. Otherwise, if the variance of y were V, the variance of $\frac{1}{2}(y + y)$ would be $V/2$, i.e. by doubling y and halving again, we could reduce its variance! This ridiculous result, arising because y is not uncorrelated with itself, shows how important is the requirement that the ys must be uncorrelated.

Means and Variances

is $(30 \cdot 6 - 29 \cdot 0) = 1 \cdot 6$, and its variance is the sum of the variances of the means, i.e. $(1 \cdot 20/5 + 1 \cdot 20/3) = 0 \cdot 64$. This is, in fact, the expression $(s^2/N_1 + s^2/N_2)$, or $s^2(1/N_1 + 1/N_2)$, which appears in the formula for t to test the difference between two means. The standard error of the difference is the square root of its variance, i.e. $\sqrt{0 \cdot 64}$ or $0 \cdot 80$. Thus, the difference between the male and female means $(1 \cdot 6)$ is exactly twice its standard error of $0 \cdot 80$. The basic steps are always the same:

(1) calculate the 'residual' mean square,
(2) use the rules, given above, to calculate the variance of some interesting combination of the original ys (in this case, the difference between the two means),
(3) take the square root of that variance to find the standard error.

One-way table

Suppose we have done an experiment involving a single set of different treatments, i.e. to every y value there is assigned one, and only one, treatment. We have just considered an example with two treatments, namely male and female. But now suppose that there are several treatments. The data form a 'one-way table', because they are classified into a single set of treatments and so could be written in a single row, divided according to those treatments. For example, the data in Example 2 of this chapter could be written: $1 \cdot 07 \ 1 \cdot 20 \ 0 \cdot 98 \ 1 \cdot 07$ ‖ $1 \cdot 20 \ 1 \cdot 31 \ 1 \cdot 36 \ 1 \cdot 27$ ‖ $1 \cdot 35 \ 1 \cdot 41 \ 1 \cdot 40 \ 4 \cdot 37 \ 1 \cdot 36 \ 1 \cdot 39$. The analysis follows the principles stated in Chapter 1. The over-all mean is sub-tracted from each observation, and the sum of squares of the remainders is the 'original sum of squares, corrected for the mean'. Then, individual 'treatment' means are used to calculate a new set of residuals, whose sum of squares is the 'residual sum of squares'. The difference between those two sums of squares is the 'sum of squares due to fitting separate treatment means', or 'treatments sum of squares' for short. It is concerned, as before, with the *differences* among the set of treatments.

Now we wish to compare the set of 'treatment' means. If we choose the biggest and the smallest means, just because they *are* the biggest and smallest, they will quite possibly appear significantly different, as judged by a t-test; but that conclusion may well be spurious. The biggest and smallest values chosen from a set of random numbers may also appear to be significantly different, until we remember that they have been specially chosen from the whole set of numbers. There is therefore a danger of drawing unjustified conclusions, when comparing a set of 'treatment' means. True, there are special multiple-range tests (discussed in Chapter 6) designed to avoid that danger. But the examination of a set of 'treatment' means requires not only statistical tests, but also common sense and biological 'gumption'. We have to bear in mind the biological story, as well as the statistical significance. No amount of statistical manipulation can relieve us of responsibility for the biological conclusions which we draw from the data.

It is possible to make numerous comparisons between a set of 'treatment' means. Some of those comparisons will answer questions which the biologist would have wanted to ask *before* he did the experiment. It is always valid to make an appropriate significance test on any such comparison, but other comparisons are interesting, not *a priori*, but because the data themselves suggest some unanticipated effect. There is then a danger of mistaking chance differences for real biological effects; but, at the other extreme, it is possible to ignore unexpected differences which, the data insist, are really there. The following rule, although not foolproof, makes a useful guide. Suppose the variance ratio ('treatments' mean square/'residual' mean square) is not significant, suggesting that there are no differences among the set of treatments as a whole. There may still be one or two individual differences which have been submerged, when ploughed in with the other treatment means; the differences, although really there, not being big enough to significantly inflate the 'between-treatments' mean square. In that case, *a priori* comparisons, decided on before the experiment was done, may be made with confidence; but it would be very dangerous to rely on apparent differences which jump to notice only when the data are inspected. On the other hand, if the variance ratio indicates that some real differences exist between treatments, we may not only make *a priori* comparisons, but also have more confidence in unanticipated differences. It is still wise not to put too much trust in such unexpected conclusions, but merely regard them as interesting suggestions for further experimentation. Now suppose the treatments can be arranged in order *a priori*, e.g. they might represent increasing doses of a fertilizer. Then the 'treatment' means may show a genuine pattern, e.g. they may increase steadily as the fertilizer dose increases, even though the differences between consecutive means may not be 'significant'.

There are innumerable different comparisons which can be made between a set of means, but those comparisons are not all independent of each other. Suppose that, in some experiment, the mean of the first treatment has, by chance, come out rather too big. Then the value of $\bar{y}_1 - \bar{y}_2$ will be too big, and so will $\bar{y}_1 - \bar{y}_3$. If the difference $\bar{y}_1 - \bar{y}_2$ is mistakenly judged to be 'significant', it is quite likely that $\bar{y}_1 - \bar{y}_3$ will also appear to be 'significant'. That does not mean that we may not test both $\bar{y}_1 - \bar{y}_2$ and $\bar{y}_1 - \bar{y}_3$ if we want to, but we should remember that the two comparisons are not independent. Fortunately, it is often the over-all pattern of the whole set of means that is interesting, rather than any particular comparison between individual means. It is usually quite sufficient to calculate the set of treatment means with their standard errors, and inspect them carefully to draw appropriate biological conclusions. That is why it is so important to grasp the rules, discussed earlier in this chapter, for handling means, standard deviations, variances, and standard errors.

Suppose that there are real differences between treatments, and that an over-all mean is required for the whole set of treatments. If one treatment is represented by more y values than another treatment, the over-all grand mean will favour the first treatment, as compared with the second. To avoid bias, it may be advisable to take the unweighted mean of the individual 'treatment' means (Example 1, this chapter). Such a mean would be less precise (i.e. have a bigger standard error) than the over-all mean, but would avoid the possibility of bias. The difficulty does not arise if every treatment has the same number of y observations.

'Nested' one-way table

A 'nested' (or hierarchical) classification is a simple extension of a one-way table. Some or all of the treatments in the one-way table are subdivided into sub-treatments. For example, the ordinary Linnaean nomenclature is hierarchical; the generic name is the treatment, and the specific name is the sub-treatment. Each species (sub-treatment) belongs to only one genus (treatment). Example 3 of this chapter shows the detailed analysis of a 'nested' table. The student would be wise to work through Examples 1–3, before attempting the complexities of a two-way table.

Two-way table

Until now, we have considered only a single set of treatments. For example, an animal may belong to one species or another, but not to two at once. Now suppose that there are two sets of treatments, superimposed on each other. The y values are classified simultaneously into 'rows' and 'columns'. Each row represents one particular treatment from the first set of treatments, and each column represents a treatment from the second set. It is no longer possible to display the data in a single line and still show the structure of the treatments: instead, a two-dimensional array is necessary. If our dogs, besides being male and female, may be of different breeds, we might have a two-way table as follows.

	Alsatian	Borzoi	Collie	Dingo
Male				
Female				

The two sets of treatments cut across each other, because a male can belong to any breed, and an Alsatian may be of either sex. It is this circumstance that distinguishes a two-way table from a 'nested' one-way table. In the one-way table, once the species is known, the genus follows automatically; in the two-way table, both breed and sex must be specified.

In a two-way table, each particular combination of a row and a column is called a 'cell'. Each value of y is assigned to its appropriate cell. If the number of observations per cell is the same in every cell, the table is 'orthogonal' (although tables may also be orthogonal in some other circumstances). Orthogonality has nothing to do with the actual values of y, but with the pattern of frequencies in the cells.

The analysis is based on the assumption that

$$y_{ij} = m + a_i + b_j + \text{interaction} + \text{remainder}. \qquad (2.1)$$

This means that any value of y in the cell formed by row i and column j is the sum of the following.

(1) An over-all constant m, which applies to all values of y in the table. If the table is orthogonal, m equals the over-all mean of y; otherwise, m is corrected to allow for the fact that some rows (and columns) would be represented in the over-all mean, more frequently than others.

(2) A row constant a_i, which applies to all values of y in row i. If any arbitrary constant were added to m, and the same constant subtracted from every a_i, eqn (2.1), as it stands, would be

17

unaffected. In other words, some of the constants in eqn (2.1), as it stands, are superfluous. To avoid this ambiguity, it is usual to require, quite arbitrarily, that the values of a shall add up to zero, i.e. the average value of all the as is zero. Then, m takes care of the over-all average, while the as are concerned with *differences* between rows.

(3) A column constant b_j, which applies to all the values of y in column j. The average value of all the bs is similarly set equal to the arbitrary value zero. The analysis is symmetrical for rows and columns, i.e. interchanging rows and columns will produce exactly the same analysis, but with row and column constants interchanged.

(4) An interaction which applies to all values of y in the cell (i, j). The term 'interaction' is used here in a purely statistical sense. If rows and columns interact, it means that the difference between two rows is not always the same, but depends to some extent on the particular choice of column; and vice versa. An interaction may sometimes be regarded as a statistical parameter in its own right (like m, a_i, and b_j), but it is usually preferable to regard it as 'a bit left over after the additive terms m, a_i, and b_j have done their best'. The interactions are really a measure of the failure of the purely additive model

$$y_{ij} = m + a_i + b_j$$

to describe the data completely. If interactions occur, that additive model is not a perfect way of viewing the situation. It might be possible to find some transformation of y to a new scale of measurement (Chap. 5) which eliminates interactions, so that the row- and column- treatments act together in perfectly additive fashion on the new scale. That would be advantageous from a statistical point of view, it being much easier to think about the situation when there are no interactions.

(5) A remainder which applies only to the particular value of y, and is included because values of y in the same cell will not be all the same. If there is no more than one value of y in any cell, there will be no remainder variation. Such a situation sometimes defeats the object of the analysis, and may be overcome by reducing the number of rows and columns, by grouping together similar rows or columns.

The *analysis* of orthogonal tables is straightforward. It indicates how much the mean square is reduced by fitting a constant a_i for each row; how much it is reduced by fitting column-constants b_j, and how much it is further reduced by fitting 'interactions'. The rows account for so much of the original sum of squares, the columns for so much, and the interactions for so much, leaving so much as residual. The *interpretation* of the results is more complicated. Some people say that the interpretation will vary according to whether we consider rows and columns to have 'fixed' or 'random' effects (the terms are explained in Chapter 4). Other people think that the distinction between 'fixed' and 'random' is inappropriate, misleading, or confused. It is certain that, in practice, the distinction makes no great difference to the answer; if it did, we could not believe that answer, anyway. The following method of interpretation may safely be used in all cases. Any mean square in the analysis of variance may be compared with the 'remainder' mean square. The appropriate significance test is the variance-ratio (or F-) test. For example, if we test the 'rows' mean square against the 'remainder' mean square, we are asking, 'Are there apparent differences between rows?' But suppose there are genuine interactions between rows and columns; that means that the effects of rows are not exactly constant, but vary slightly from column to column, and vice versa. Usually, the average row- and column-effects are bigger than the inter-actions, in which case it is useful to think in terms of average row- and column- effects, while recognizing that, to some extent, they interact. Occasionally, however, the row- and column-effects are no larger than their interactions. In this case, the additive analysis is rather pointless, since the data are really saying that the model given by eqn (2.1) is not a helpful way of viewing the situation, the difference between two rows depending entirely on the particular column involved. Instead of thinking in terms of average row- and column-effects, we may just as well treat each row—column combination as an individual treatment (unless some more appropriate, non-additive model can be used, instead of that given by eqn (2.1), to specify how rows and columns act together).

The first step in the interpretation of the analysis of variance, there-fore, is to test the 'interactions' mean square against the 'remainder' mean square. If those two mean squares are about the same size, either may be used as an estimate of residual variance. If degrees of freedom are few, a combined mean square may be calculated as follows. Add together the 'interactions' and the 'remainder' sums of squares, and divide by the sum of the corresponding degrees of freedom. (The result must lie somewhere between the 'interactions' and 'remainder' mean squares.) On the other hand, if there *are* genuine interactions, we shall need to use the 'interactions' mean square as a residual, because we shall want to ask, not 'Are there average differences between rows or columns?', but 'Are the row and column effects more important than their interactions?' So we shall then compare the 'rows' and the 'columns' mean squares with the 'interactions' mean square, rather than with the within-cell residual. (Those who know about components of variance, will realize that this may be a 'rough-and-ready' procedure, but it is usually good enough in practice.) And if there is no residual, the 'interaction' mean square must be used anyway.

The method of interpretation, just described, is based on one simple principle. To examine the reality of (say) row differences, a 'rows' mean square must be compared with some other mean square which estimates what the 'rows' mean square would be, if there were no true row effects. That principle applies, not just to two-way tables, but in all situations. An important point in experimental design is to ensure that an appropriate 'residual' mean square can indeed be estimated (Chap. 8). If we ask, 'Do row or column effects exist, regardless of their interactions?', the appropriate variance ratio is the 'rows' (or 'columns') mean square/ the within-cell 'residual' mean square. But if, as suggested, it is better to ask, 'Are row and column effects more important than their interactions?', the variance ratio becomes the 'rows' (or 'columns') mean square/the 'interactions' mean square. It can happen, although very rarely, that interactions occur between non-existent row- and column-effects. You may like to consider the implications of that situation.

Before attempting the next section, the student should make sure that he has worked through Example 4 of this chapter, which analyses an orthogonal two-way table. The next section is a complicated example of the simple principles of Chapter 1.

Non-orthogonal two-way table

The analysis of a non-orthogonal two-way table is more complex than the analysis of an orthogonal table; and its interpretation is more problematical. Whenever possible, experiments and samples should be designed to avoid non-orthogonality; but, sometimes, the biologist cannot specify in advance how many observations will be collected in each cell.

If the table is non-orthogonal, it is not possible to separate out the effects of rows and columns completely. It is easy to see why not. The average of y for one row will include the effects of some particular assortment of the columns, while another row will be associated with a different combination of the column constants. Then, however intensively we may analyse, we can never be entirely sure that an apparent difference between rows is not, to some extent, a concealed effect of columns, transmitted via the uneven pattern of cell frequencies. Vice versa, apparent differences between columns may, in part, be the second-hand effects of rows. We have to proceed as follows. Firstly, we fit row-constants only, giving the usual straightforward one-way analysis (between-rows and within-rows) which absorbs a sum of squares for rows. Then we fit row- and column-constants simultaneously, absorbing a sum of squares for rows and columns together. The difference between those two sums of squares is the *extra* sum of squares absorbed by columns, after the row-constants have been fitted. It is called the 'sum of squares for columns, adjusted for rows'; this is abbreviated as 'columns adj. rows'. It must represent the effects of columns only, since all the effects of rows have already been accounted for. It need not, however, show the *whole* effect of columns, because, as mentioned above, the 'rows' sum of squares may include some indirect effects of columns which show up in the row means. In this way, we have split the sum of squares for rows and columns together, into 'sum of squares for rows' and 'sum of squares for columns adj. rows'. We now start again, and split the same sum of squares for rows and columns together, into 'sum of squares for columns' and 'sum of squares for rows adj. columns'. This double split is the best we can do, to divide the variance of y into a part for 'rows' and a part for 'columns'. If the table were orthogonal, the split would be clean and unambiguous, the 'sum of squares for columns' would be the same as the 'sum of squares for columns adj. rows', and the 'sum of squares for rows' would equal the 'sum of squares for rows adj. columns'. Orthogonal tables may be recognized in that way. The fact that the split cannot be made unambiguously, unless the table is orthogonal, is the main reason for designing experiments to avoid non-orthogonality, wherever possible. (Another reason is to get as much information as possible for our money.) Orthogonal tables may be analysed, if necessary, by desk calculator; but the analysis of a non-orthogonal table is very laborious (except where there are only two rows or two columns), and needs to be done by computer.

We may now go on to see if there are genuine effects of rows and columns. If both 'rows' and 'rows adj. columns' mean squares are significantly large, it means that there are real row effects; but it can happen, that the 'rows' mean square is large, but the 'rows adj. columns' mean square is not. (That cannot happen in an orthogonal table, where those two mean squares are necessarily identical.) That means that there are apparent row effects which *might* be the indirect effects of columns. We cannot be certain. All we can say is that the observed row effects *can* be explained away as the indirect effects of columns. It is unusual, although not impossible, for very large row effects to be indirect effects of columns. If neither 'rows' nor 'rows adj. columns' is significant, the implication is that there are no true effects of rows, so far as the data go. It sometimes happens that a mean square is large enough to suggest that there may be some effect, but not large enough to insist that the effect is certainly there. In that case, it helps to look at the pattern of values of the row constants a_i, to see if they make sense biologically. As in any other analysis, the mechanical use of significance tests cannot absolve the biologist from responsibility for his interpretation.

Sometimes, a two-way table is designed to be orthogonal, but one or two values are accidentally missing. Before the advent of computers, special 'missing-value' techniques were used to analyse such tables as if they were truly orthogonal. Such techniques, if used properly, must necessarily give the same answer as the appropriate non-orthogonal analysis. These days, we simply do the non-orthogonal analysis by computer. Since the table is very nearly orthogonal, there is very little ambiguity in its interpretation.

Three (or more) -way tables are analysed following the same principles as we have used for two-way tables. The interpretation of a seriously non-orthogonal three-way table can be a nightmare of ambiguity.

Presentation of results

The presentation of results is largely a matter of personal preference. Unfortunately, editors and referees of biological journals often insist on unnecessary statistical detail. Sprent (1970) castigates 'misguided editors who think that all numerical results can be made respectable by quoting significant differences or significance levels — often denoted by * or ** or ***, a symbolism more appropriate to a hotel guide-book than a serious scientific paper'. There is, regrettably, often a sharp distinction between statistical analysis performed to find an answer, and that done for publication. Frequently, elaborate statistical analyses are presented to prove points which are perfectly obvious. (That is not to say that statistical analyses should not be included in a biological paper, but that they should only appear when necessary and relevant.) There are two considerations here. Firstly, it is important to supply the reader with enough detail, so that he can, if he thinks fit, draw different conclusions from the same data. On the other hand, the more tables of numbers there are in a paper, the fewer people will read it. Very often, a table of 'treatment' means and standard errors is all that is necessary. If all the means have the same standard error, it need be quoted only once; if the means all have *approximately* the same standard error, an average standard error is usually good enough. However, if the means have very different accuracies, it is necessary to indicate the accuracy of each mean, either by quoting its own standard error or, perhaps, by showing the number of observations on which that mean is based (together with some over-all estimate of variability). In biology, it is rarely worth quoting more than three significant figures in any mean; if someone says 'a duck lays 4·603 eggs, on average', the final figure 3 is almost certainly worthless. However, it is useful to quote one more decimal place in the standard error than in the mean itself, because that helps to preserve accuracy in subsequent calculations (e.g. of confidence limits). Given the means and standard errors, it is possible to deduce all sorts of calculations (e.g. analysis of variance, significance tests, confidence limits); whereas it is not possible to calculate backwards from a 'significance probability' to a standard error. It must be clearly stated that quoted standard errors *are* standard errors, rather than, say, standard deviations or confidence intervals. The enthusiastic starring of significance levels, although very popular, is inadvisable, because it betrays a misunderstanding of the nature of a significance test (Chap. 6). It is much easier to look at a picture, graph, or histogram, than to examine a table of numbers. So it is a good idea to present results pictorially, where suitable. Usually, however, information cannot be stated so accurately on a graph as in numerical form. And it can cost even more to print a figure than to print a table of numbers.

Examples 2

(As far as possible, Examples should be worked using a computer.)

(1) (To be done twice, once by desk calculator and once by computer.) A sample of eight Loch Ness monsters was found to contain five males and three females. Their lengths (in feet) were

Means and Variances

Males	Females
39	28
40	30
37	29
39	
38	

Do a one-way analysis of variance. Find the mean of each sex, the over-all sample mean, the average of the male and female means, and the difference between the male and female means. Estimate the variances of those five quantities.

(2) Average growth rates (cm/day) of three lots of pigs were as follows.

Lot 1 Large White	Lot 2 Landrace	Lot 3 Large White x Landrace
1·07	1·20	1·35
1·20	1·31	1·41
0·98	1·36	1·40
1·07	1·27	4·37
		1·36
		1·39

Calculate means m_1, m_2, and m_3 (with standard errors) for each lot. Calculate $m_2 - m_1$, $m_3 - m_2$, and $m_3 - \frac{1}{2}m_1 - \frac{1}{2}m_2$ together with their standard errors. What is the point of making these particular comparisons?

(3) A 'nested' (or hierarchical) classification. A set of sparrows nests each contained three chicks. Extra food was given to the parents of some nests, not to others. The chicks were weighed at ten-day intervals. Gains in weight(g) of each chick were as follows.

Treatment	Nest number	Weight gains
Control (no extra food)	1	1·6, 2·0, 2·0
	2	0·8, 0·7, 0·3
	3	1·2, 1·9, 1·5
	4	0·5, 0·8, 1·4
	5	1·3, 0·2, 1·0
Extra food	6	1·6, 1·7, 2·1
	7	2·2, 2·0, 2·2
	8	2·4, 1·6, 2·2
	9	1·3, 1·9, 1·9
	10	2·0, 2·4, 1·7

Compare the average weight gains of chicks in the two treatments.

(4) Sprinting speeds (ft s^{-1}) of various animals were as follows.

	Cheetah	Greyhound	Kangaroo
Males	56, 52, 55	37, 33, 40	44, 48, 47
Females	53, 50, 51	38, 42, 41	39, 41, 36

Analyse and interpret this two-way table.

(5). To be done only by computer, using a program for analysing a two-way non-orthogonal table. Quantities of beer (pints) drunk in a contest by various individuals were as follows.

Australians (male)	12·3, 14·0, 11·5, 9·7, 11·4, 10·8
British (male)	10·4, 12·5
British (female)	7·8, 7·0, 5·9, 6·0
Germans (male)	10·0, 11·0, 12·0
Germans (female)	6·0, 7·0, 7·0

(a) Do a one-way analysis of nationalities, pooling sexes; what is your conclusion? (b) Do a two-way analysis of both nationality and sex; does this analysis modify the previous conclusion?

(6) What would your interpretation be if, in a non-orthogonal two-way table, the 'columns' and 'rows adj. columns' mean squares were both large, but the 'rows' mean square was not?

(7) Show that, in a two-way table, the 'sum of squares for rows and columns together', i.e. the sum of squares accounted for by fitting row- and column-constants simultaneously, cannot be less than the 'sum of squares for rows', even though the actual row-constants may be different in the two cases, and, therefore, that the sum of squares for 'columns adjusted for rows' cannot be negative.

(8) If y has mean m and variance V, show that the average value of y^2 is $m^2 + V$. From Example 3 (Chap. 1) $\Sigma(y - \bar{y})^2 = \Sigma y^2 - N\bar{y}^2$. Show that the average value of $\Sigma(y - \bar{y})^2$ is $(N - 1)V$. Therefore, if the sum of squares $\Sigma(y - \bar{y})^2$ is divided by its degrees of freedom $N - 1$, the mean square estimates V, whatever the value of m may be. What happens if $N = 1$? Show that the original mean square $\Sigma y^2/N$ over-estimates V, unless $m = 0$.

(9) *Finite population.* The formulae for standard errors, given in this chapter, assume that the population is infinite. For example, the population of 'all possible Australian beer-drinkers' is so large that it is effectively infinite. However, now suppose that the population is small. The sampling fraction f is the ratio of sample size to population size. For an infinite population, f must be zero. If $f = 1$, the sample contains

Means and Variances

the whole population; the population still has a standard deviation, but the sample mean is precisely the population mean, and so its standard error is zero. In general, the variance of the sample mean is $V(1 - f)/N$. For an infinite population, $f = 0$, and the variance of the sample mean becomes V/N as usual.

(10) *Weighted analysis.* If the variance of y is obviously not constant, and the trouble cannot be dealt with by transformation (Chap. 5), a weighted analysis may be necessary. If the variance of y_i is V_i, the weight w_i given to y_i is $1/V_i$. The weighted mean $\bar{y}$ is then $\Sigma w_i y_i / \Sigma w_i$. Using the rule given in this chapter, prove that the variance of $\bar{y}$ is $1/\Sigma w_i$. Show that this reduces (as it must) to V/N when every $V_i = V$.

A warning — if variances estimated from different mean squares are used to calculate weights, the weighted mean $\bar{y}$ may be biased by the inaccuracy of estimation of the variances.

(11) This example uses the rules for weighted analysis used in Example 10 to analyse the non-orthogonal table of Example 5. The within-cells 'remainder' mean square is 1·373. The average difference (male—female) for the British is

$$\left(\frac{10\cdot4 + 12\cdot5}{2} - \frac{7\cdot8 + 7\cdot0 + 5\cdot9 + 6\cdot0}{4} \right)$$

with variance $1\cdot373 \left(\frac{1}{2} + \frac{1}{4} \right)$, i.e. it is 4·775 with variance 1·0298, and, therefore, with weight $1/1\cdot0298 = 0\cdot9711$. Similarly, the average difference (male—female) for Germans is 4·333 with weight 1·0925. There is no Australian comparison, because Australian women are not allowed in public bars. The weighted average difference is, therefore, $(0\cdot9711 \times 4\cdot775 + 1\cdot0925 \times 4\cdot333)/(0\cdot9711 + 1\cdot0925) = 4\cdot541$ with variance $1/(0\cdot9711 + 1\cdot0925) = 0\cdot4846$. This estimate of sex difference has excluded nationalities, i.e. it is 'sexes adj. nationalities'. It is shown in Chapter 6 that t^2 must equal F when both ask the same question. Compare the value of t, i.e. $4\cdot541/\sqrt{0\cdot4846}$, with the variance ratio 'sexes adj. nationalities'/remainder, in the analysis of variance of Example 5. How can you obtain a value of t corresponding to the variance ratio interactions/remainder?

3 | REGRESSION, CORRELATION, AND DETERMINATION

CHAPTER 1 discussed the use of some function F_i — which might be a mean, a regression, or any other suitable function — to predict the value of y_i. In Chapter 2, the emphasis shifted, so that we considered means as entities in their own right. This chapter considers regressions in the same way.

The estimation of means may be considered as a special case of regression. Suppose we have a one-way table of values of y. For example, y might be the milk yield of a cow, and the 'treatments' might be different breeds, e.g. Friesian, Guernsey, Jersey, and Shorthorn. To estimate the average yield of each breed, we use the model

$$y = \text{the appropriate treatment mean} + \text{remainder.} \qquad (3.1)$$

We shall now create 'dummy variates' x, one for each breed. Usually, a variate is something we measure, e.g., the live weight of a cow. However, a dummy variate is something quite arbitrary; we ourselves decide what its values shall be. In this case, we use it to code for a breed of cow. The assigned value of x_1 is 1 for all Friesian cows, and 0 for cows of any other breed. The assigned value of x_2 is 1 for Guernseys, and 0 for any other breed. Similarly x_3 and x_4 indicate Jerseys and Shorthorns. It follows that if a cow is Friesian, it has $x_1 = 1$ and $x_2 = x_3 = x_4 = 0$; if Guernsey, it has $x_2 = 1$ and $x_1 = x_3 = x_4 = 0$; and so on. Then eqn (3.1) can be rewritten

$$y = b_1 x_1 + b_2 x_2 + b_3 x_3 + b_4 x_4 + \text{remainder.} \qquad (3.2)$$

Since $x_1 = 1$ and $x_2 = x_3 = x_4 = 0$ for Friesians, eqn (3.2) becomes $y = b_1 + \text{remainder}$ for Friesians, i.e. b_1 is the Friesian mean. Similarly b_2 is the Guernsey mean, and so on. Now eqn (3.2) is the basic equation for multiple regression. If we fed the variates y and x_1, x_2, x_3, x_4 into a multiple-regression program, we should get values of b_1, b_2, b_3, b_4 identical with the sample means for each breed. We should be doing the same analysis by a different method, and so we must get the same answer. Dummy variates are mentioned for two reasons. Firstly, they show that there is no intrinsic difference between the fitting of means and the fitting of regressions. (It is true that, in a regression, the x-variate can usually take a *continuous* range of values, whereas we fit means to *discrete* categories, e.g. Friesians or Guernseys, so that the dummy x-variates in eqn (3.2) take discrete values 0 and 1, but that makes no difference to the regression analysis itself.) Secondly, as we shall see, dummy variates are occasionally used in practice. Usually, we calculate means directly, because they require much less computation than does a multiple regression. But, sometimes, when dealing with a lot of non-orthogonal cross-treatments, it saves trouble to actually use dummy x-variates (assuming that you have an adequate multiple-regression program).

The simplest regression equation, a straight line of slope b, is

$$y = bx + \text{remainder}. \qquad (3.3)$$

This equation deliberately contains no intercept. If $x = 0$, y will, on average, be zero, i.e. the regression line goes through the origin. To estimate b, we minimize the 'residual' sum of squares $\Sigma(y - bx)^2$. Elementary calculus shows that b is estimated as $\Sigma xy / \Sigma x^2$. The values of Σxy and Σx^2 are calculated from the original values of the xs and ys. This is the case (mentioned in Chapter 1) where neither y nor x is corrected for the mean, as a first step in the analysis. Consequently, the analysis of variance of y includes no correction for the mean.

Usually, however, we include an intercept a to obtain the ordinary linear regression of y on a single x-variate

$$y = a + bx + \text{remainder}. \qquad (3.4)$$

Strictly speaking, since eqn (3.4) contains *two* coefficients, it could be regarded as a regression on *two* x-variates, one of which is x itself (with coefficient b), and the other a dummy variate (coefficient a) which always takes the value 1. But since, in practice, it is very simple to estimate the extra parameter a, we call eqn (3.4) a single regression. It can be shown that to minimize $\Sigma(y - a - bx)^2$ is equivalent to minimizing $\Sigma[(y - \bar{y}) - b(x - \bar{x})]^2$. Therefore, b is estimated as $\Sigma(x - \bar{x})(y - \bar{y}) / \Sigma(x - \bar{x})^2$, i.e. the analysis is much the same as for the model of eqn (3.3), except that both x and y are corrected for their respective means. In other words, b is calculated, not from x and y as such, but from their deviations from the mean. In practice, eqn (3.4) is almost always used in preference to eqn (3.3). Suppose we are concerned with the regression of body weight on body length in adult sheep. It is true that a sheep of zero length would have zero weight, i.e. the regression must theoretically go through the origin. However, we cannot expect the relation between weight and length to be a straight line, over the whole range of lengths from zero to adult size; whereas it may, or may not, be possible to describe the relation by a straight line *not* through the origin, over the range of adult sizes which concern us. We need insist that a regression line must go through the origin only when the values of y and x actually extend down towards zero. Throughout this chapter, we assume that the relation between y and x is, over the range of values in the sample, a straight line. Chapters 4 and 13 deal with problems of non-linearity.

Regression is essentially a method for predicting y from x. For example, the weights of eye lenses are sometimes used to estimate the ages of wild animals, because the growth of the eye lens is not greatly affected by environmental disturbances. Obviously, the size of the eye lens depends on the age of the animal, rather than vice versa, and so it might seem appropriate to regress lens weight on age. But we want to predict the animals' ages from their lens weights; for that purpose, we need to regress age on lens weight. In general, the regression lines of y on x, and of x on y, are different. That need cause us no difficulty; it means that the best formulae for predicting y from x, and x from y, are not the same.

Regression is used to *predict* y from x. That is, most often, precisely what we want to do, even when it might seem, at first sight, that we really want to *describe* the biological relation between y and x. Sometimes, however, we know in advance that there will be a linear 'functional relation' between two variates, and we wish to estimate the parameters (a and b) of that relation. We cannot often be sure, in biology, that the relation will be truly linear; but, for example, we can expect enzyme activity to be directly proportional to enzyme concentration, over a certain range of values. We know that there are *two* regression lines, that of y on x (predicting y from x) and that of x on y (predicting x from y), but there can be only *one* underlying functional relation. How can we find it? A difficulty arises because of errors of measurement. Suppose the observed values y and x differ from the true biological values Y and X by unavoidable errors of measurement, e.g. we cannot measure the true enzyme concentration exactly. At one extreme, the errors of measurement are zero, in which case the values of $y(= Y)$ and $x(= X)$ must lie exactly on the straight line 'functional relation', and both regression lines will coincide with the functional relation. At the other extreme, errors of measurement will be large, so that the regression of y on x gives poor predictions of y, yet the underlying relation between Y and X remains untouched. The technical problems of estimating a functional relation are discussed in the next paragraph. They do not affect the normal use of regression to predict y from x, so the next paragraph may be omitted by the student if he wishes.

The true values X and Y exactly obey the equation

$$Y = A + BX.$$

We want to find A and B, but we do not know the values of the Xs and Ys. The regression coefficient b of y on x is $\Sigma(y - \bar{y})(x - \bar{x})/\Sigma(x - \bar{x})^2$. Suppose the sample size is N, and the variance of the errors of x is V. It can be shown that $\Sigma(y - \bar{y})(x - \bar{x})$ will, on average, equal $\Sigma(Y - \bar{Y})(X - \bar{X})$, but $\Sigma(x - \bar{x})^2$ will, on average, equal $\Sigma(X - \bar{X})^2 + (N - 1)V$, and so the regression coefficient of y on x is

$$b = \frac{\Sigma(y - \bar{y})(x - \bar{x})}{\Sigma(x - \bar{x})^2} \cong \frac{\Sigma(Y - \bar{Y})(X - \bar{X})}{\Sigma(X - \bar{X})^2 + (N - 1)V} .$$

But the unknown value B is $\Sigma(Y - \bar{Y})(X - \bar{X})/\Sigma(X - \bar{X})^2$. Unless $V = 0$, the denominator of b, i.e. $\Sigma(X - \bar{X})^2 + (N - 1)V$, will exceed the denominator of B, i.e. $\Sigma(X - \bar{X})^2$, and so the absolute size of b comes out smaller than B. Unless $V = 0$, i.e. unless x is measured without error, the regression of y on x gives a diluted estimate of the slope of Y on X. So, if x is known without error, the regression of y on x estimates the functional relation between Y and X; and if y is known without error, the regression of x on y does so. But, if both x and y have errors of measurement, the line $Y = A + BX$ lies somewhere between the regression lines of y on x, and x on y. There are two practical remedies. If we can estimate V, we can correct the bias in b by subtracting $(N - 1)V$ from the denominator $\Sigma(x - \bar{x})^2$; but if we do that, we are estimating $\Sigma(X - \bar{X})^2$ as a 'component of variance', which is often rather risky (Chaps. 4 and 10). The other way of estimating B is to split the sample into two halves, one containing all the large values of x and y, and one containing all the small values, find the means $(\bar{x}, \bar{y})$ for each half, and calculate the slope of the line joining those two 'centres of gravity'. This method cannot be used on every sample. It requires that, when the sample is split into large and small values of x, it shall simultaneously split into large and small values of y. When that is not possible, or very nearly so, the method should not be used. The whole difficulty (the fact that b is a biased estimate of B) may also be avoided by the following device. An experimenter decides what the values of X shall be, and arranges the experiment accordingly. For example, X might be a desired setting of an instrument, and x the setting actually achieved. The value of x will, in general, differ from X; but as long as positive and negative errors are equally likely, it is legitimate to analyse the results with X in place of x. The fundamental point here is that the experimenter himself prescribes — and therefore knows — what X should be.

We may now return to the *predictive* use of regression. Fifty years ago, statisticians thought in terms of correlations (which treat x and y as equal partners), rather than regressions. Nowadays, we usually use regression methods, recognizing that most statistical problems are really problems of prediction. Since the x-variates are used only as 'something which will, we hope, predict y', they can be anything we choose. If they include errors of measurement, it does not matter, because any future values of x (used to predict corresponding values of y) will include similar errors of measurement. The xs need not be distributed Normally, or in any other prescribed way. The regression analysis takes the values of x for granted and minimizes the sum of squares of the *vertical* remainders (Fig. 3.1), i.e. it is concerned to make predictions of y as accurate as possible. It assumes that the remainder variance of y does not change as x changes; otherwise, a weighted analysis would be appropriate.

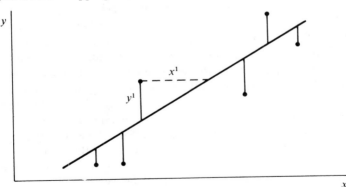

Fig. 3.1. The regression of y on x minimizes the sum of squares of the vertical remainders y^1. The regression of x on y would minimize the sum of squares of the horizontal deviations x^1.

Regression, Correlation, and Determination

We may use the rule given in Chapter 2 to calculate the standard error of the regression coefficient b. The value of b is $\Sigma(y - \bar{y})(x - \bar{x})/\Sigma(x - \bar{x})^2$. Since $\Sigma(x - \bar{x}) = 0$ by definition of $\bar{x}$, it follows that $\bar{y}\Sigma(x - \bar{x}) = 0$. Therefore, the value of b is equal to $\Sigma y(x - \bar{x})/\Sigma(x - \bar{x})^2$. That is, b is $a_1 y_1 + a_2 y_2 + \ldots$, where $a_i = (x_i - \bar{x})/\Sigma(x_i - \bar{x})^2$. It is because b is a *linear* function of the ys that regressions are 'robust' (Chap. 4). Since every y has the same remainder variance V, the variance of b is $a_1^2 V + a_2^2 V + \ldots$, which becomes $V/\Sigma(x - \bar{x})^2$. This is the usual expression for the variance of a regression coefficient. V is estimated by the 'remainder' mean square of y, and the standard error of b is the square root of its variance, i.e. $\sqrt{[V/\Sigma(x - \bar{x})^2]}$.

Sometimes we wish to compare the regression of y on x in different blocks of data. Blocks are sets of data which we wish to keep distinct, because we suspect that they might have different means $\bar{x}$ or $\bar{y}$, or different regression slopes b. Blocks might represent 'treatments' of interest (e.g. male versus female, as in a one-way table) or they might represent some unavoidable discontinuities (e.g. data collected at different places or in different years) which need to be eliminated from the analysis. We could, of course, analyse each block quite separately, but usually we analyse all the blocks together, to get a single analysis of variance with a single 'residual' mean square. We work on the usual plan, described in Chapter 1. Firstly, we ask if there is any over-all regression (within blocks), and then we fit a separate regression for each block, to see if the regression differs from block to block. The situation is complicated by the fact that a regression equation contains *two* coefficients, a and b, which can be examined separately. But we are usually more interested in the slope b, than in the intercept a. It is the slope that tells us how much change to expect in y, consequent on any given change in x. If two regression lines have different slopes, the regressions are intrinsically different. In that case, the two lines must meet somewhere, but precisely where is usually of no great interest. There is then no point in asking whether the intercepts are the same, i.e. whether the two lines meet at $x = 0$. If the slopes are different, we do not care too much about the intercepts; but if the slopes are the same, we shall want to know whether the lines are parallel (intercepts different) or identical (intercepts equal). So we proceed as follows. We correct every value of x and y for its block mean, so that average differences between blocks are eliminated. Then we calculate the over-all regression slope to see if x can predict y at all. Then we calculate a regression for each block separately, to see if the slope differs from block to block. If so, we need to use a different equation (both slope and intercept) for each block. But if the slope is approximately the same in every block, we adopt the over-all value of b, and then ask if the intercepts are different from block to block. It can happen that different slopes in different blocks cancel each other so that there is no over-all regression, but such cases are very rare in practice. All these questions may be examined by the analysis of variance of y, or equivalently by looking at the values of a and b with their standard errors.

Now suppose that different blocks have different values of $\bar{x}$ and $\bar{y}$, but the regression slope is the same in every block. Then we can, if we think it advisable, use the regression to correct the values of $\bar{y}$ for the differences in $\bar{x}$, i.e. compare the $\bar{y}$s at a standard value of $\bar{x}$, say x_0. Fig. 3.2 shows the regression in one block. Starting from the observed

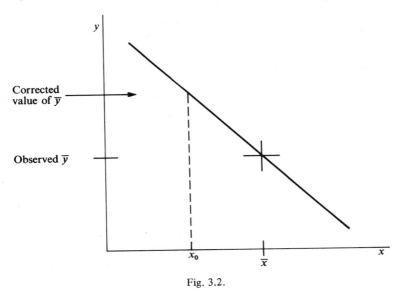

Fig. 3.2.

values $(\bar{x}, \bar{y})$, the corrected value of $\bar{y}$ is found by moving along the regression line from $x = \bar{x}$ to $x = x_0$. Since the regression slope is the same in every block, the *comparison* between the corrected values of $\bar{y}$ will be the same, whatever standard value x_0 we may use. The method should not be used when the slopes are not the same. If we use $x_0 = 0$,

Regression, Correlation, and Determination

the corrected $\bar{y}$ is simply the intercept. So if the regression lines are parallel in different blocks (intercepts different), there still remain differences between $\bar{y}$s after correction for the differences in $\bar{x}$; but if the regression lines in different blocks coincide (intercepts equal), the observed differences in $\bar{x}$ are sufficient to explain the observed differences in $\bar{y}$. Or, in other words, the between-blocks regression (of $\bar{y}$s on $\bar{x}$s) is the same as the within-blocks regression. This method (called analysis of covariance) of correcting y to a common x can be very misleading when 'blocks' refer to experimental treatments, and those treatments affect x itself, for then we are using one kind of treatment effect (on x) to correct another kind of treatment effect (on y). The procedure is only used when it is certain that the experimental treatments can have no effect on x. For example, experimental treatments cannot affect the calendar age of an animal; if x is age, differences in $\bar{x}$ between treatments cannot be due to the treatments themselves, and so it is permissible to correct y for x.

Regression analysis, like any other statistical method, can be misused. Fig. 3.3 shows two extreme cases where mechanical use of the method

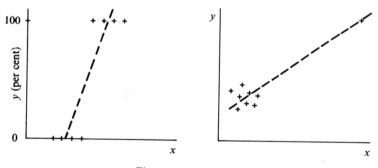

Fig. 3.3. (a) and (b).

could mislead. Fig. 3.3(a) shows a sudden jump from 0 to 100 per cent. A regression of y on x would be highly 'significant', but it would not represent the true relation between y and x. In Fig. 3.3(b), there is clearly something unusual about the single outstanding point. It might even be erroneous, yet it largely determines the position of the regression line. It would be dangerous to use the regression in Fig. 3.3(b) to interpolate for intermediate values of x, since there is no evidence that the relation between x and y is truly linear. Unless there is some theory which specifies what the relation between y and x should look like, we can never safely extrapolate any regression, however well estimated, beyond the observed range of xs. Fig. 3.3 shows how important it can be to plot things graphically. It is much easier to detect irregularities in a graph or histogram than in sets of written numbers.

It would be wise for the student to make sure that he can do Examples 1–3, before going on to multiple regression.

Multiple regression, of y on several xs, uses the equation

$$y = a + b_1 x_1 + b_2 x_2 + \ldots + \text{remainder.} \tag{3.5}$$

Eqn (3.5) is the same as eqn (3.2) except that it includes an intercept a. Once again, the primary purpose is to predict y from the xs. If the xs are not correlated among themselves, the multiple regression is a straightforward combination of all the single regressions of y on each x, the coefficients b in eqn (3.5) are the same as the single coefficients in eqn (3.4), and the multiple regression accounts for a sum of squares of y equal to the total of the 'regression' sums of squares of all the single regressions. That situation would be analogous to the orthogonal two-way table (Chap. 2), where the 'rows' sum of squares and 'columns' sum of squares add up to give the 'rows + columns' sum of squares. In real life, the xs are themselves correlated; it does not matter whether their correlations are 'significant' or not. Then, the multiple regression has to allow for the correlations between the xs. The situation is analogous to a non-orthogonal two-way table, where we have to 'adjust' rows for columns (and vice versa), and where the 'rows + columns' sum of squares is not the total of the straight 'rows' columns' sums of squares. The multiple regression coefficients b in eqn (3.5) are no longer the same as the single coefficients b in eqn (3.4), and the multiple regression accounts for a sum of squares of y which is not the total of the 'regression' sums of squares of all the single regressions. An extreme case would be that two x-variates, x_1 and x_2, were always identical (correlation coefficient = 1), in which case a multiple regression of y on x_1 and x_2 could give no better prediction of y than a single regression on either x_1 or x_2, and so the sum of squares of y absorbed by the multiple regression would be no bigger than the sum of squares for the single regression. In any case, whatever the xs may be, the multiple regression of eqn (3.5) chooses the bs which give the best (linear) prediction of y from that particular set of xs.

We can usually ensure that a two-way table shall be orthogonal. A non-orthogonal two-way table is a rarity that is best avoided, wherever

Regression, Correlation, and Determination

possible. In a multiple regression, however, we usually cannot ensure that the xs shall be completely uncorrelated, and so, in practice, multiple regressions are nearly always complicated by correlations between the xs.

Suppose we wish to investigate the regression relations between numerous variates. There will be a vast number of possible regressions. The choice of which regressions to look at will be dictated by the biological questions to be asked. Now that computers have made it easy to produce multiple regressions *ad nauseam*, it is very important to keep those biological questions clearly in mind. But suppose we have chosen a y-variate for biological reasons, and suppose there are numerous possible x-variates which might be used to predict y. We may wish to find the smallest possible subset of the xs which can predict y as accurately as can the whole set of xs. In theory, we might try all possible combinations (each x absent or present); but, in practice, there are too many possible combinations, if there are more than about six xs. Sometimes there are biological considerations which recommend some xs above others, or some xs may be easier to measure than others. If not, two different sets of xs are equally acceptable, if they predict y equally well. There are no hard-and-fast rules for choosing trial combinations of xs; the job is a matter of judgement and common-sense. Two common methods are 'stripping down' (where we start with the regression on all the xs together, and step-by-step remove the 'smallest' x-variate, i.e. that x-variate which contributes least to the regression) and 'building up' (where we start with no xs, and step-by-step add in the 'best' x-variate). As always, the 'remainder' mean square tells us how much of the original variance of y remains unaccounted for by the regression. When stripping down, we know the size of the 'remainder' mean square, when all xs are included in the regression, and so we stop removing x-variates when the 'remainder' mean square seriously increases. When 'building up', we stop adding xs when the 'remainder' mean square no longer decreases seriously. Unless the xs are themselves all uncorrelated, there is no guarantee that either method will lead to the optimum combination of xs. The order in which xs are included, when building up, often differs from the order in which they are removed during stripping down — one process is not, in practice, the reverse of the other. That is because, unless the xs are uncorrelated, each x does not account for a unique amount of the variance of y. The importance of any x depends, to some extent, on which other xs have been included in the regression. (When stripping down, it is safe to discard any x

whose regression coefficient is less than its standard error, but only one such variate at a time, because removal of one unimportant x-variate may make another one important.)

The essential criterion, used to judge the success of a regression, is the reduction it achieves in the 'residual' mean square; but to *test* that reduction, we have to use the variance ratio of 'regression' mean square to 'residual' mean square (Chap. 1). Now suppose we wish to test the significance of the *extra* prediction achieved by including an extra x-variate. For example, is the regression on x_1, x_3, and x_4 better than on x_1 and x_4 alone? We use the method of Chapter 1, taking the regression on x_1 and x_4 for granted. That is, we analyse the sum of squares of y, remaining after the regression on x_1 and x_4, into two parts; the 'remainder' sum of squares after regression on x_1, x_3, and x_4 and the 'sum of squares absorbed by the extra regression on x_3, after x_1 and x_4 have been fitted'. The variance-ratio (or F-) test then compares the two mean squares. Similarly, if we want to test whether the regression on x_1, x_3, and x_4 is significantly better than regression on x_1, x_2, and x_4, we must compare the 'sum of squares absorbed by the extra regression on x_3, after x_1 and x_4 have been fitted' with the 'sum of squares absorbed by the extra regression on x_2, after x_1 and x_4 have been fitted'. Since those two sums of squares have only one degree of freedom each, their variance ratio will have to be very large before significance is established. But, when examining regressions, it often is not necessary to do significance tests; the behaviour of the 'residual' mean square reveals the whole story. Sometimes we wish to see if a multiple regression is the same in several blocks of data. The principle is the same as before. Does it pay us to fit a separate regression for each block? Since the coefficients of a multiple regression are inter-related, it is rather meaningless to test the homogeneity of any one coefficient on its own. Rather, we test the homogeneity of the whole set of regression coefficients.

Some people use multiple regression, not to predict y, but to identify those xs which determine y. This demands the greatest caution. If the data are observational, rather than experimental, there can be *no* guarantee that any observed relation is cause-and-effect (Chap. 8). If it were known in advance that a given set of xs determines y, multiple regression might be used to assess the relative importance of those xs, with three provisos.

(1) As discussed above, errors of measurement of x tend to dilute the true size of the 'functional relation'.

37

(2) *All* the important xs must be included in the analysis; if one is missing, and if it is correlated with some of the other xs, those other xs will tend to fill the gap, so giving an erroneous idea of their own direct importance.

(3) The regression analysis is based on eqn (3.5), which assumes that the effects of the xs are linear and additive. If those assumptions are wrong, the analysis will wrongly estimate the relation between y and xs (Chap. 4).

The difficulties are even greater when we do not know in advance, which xs will determine y. In Chapter 2, we saw that if a two-way table is not orthogonal, it is impossible to sort out the effects of rows and columns completely. Precisely the same difficulty occurs in multiple regression unless the xs are uncorrelated. The coefficient b of any x depends on which other xs are included in the analysis. It is always possible that the inclusion of some x which has not actually been measured could profoundly alter the coefficients of the existing regression equation. Tukey (1954) discusses the whole question at length. As he says, 'it is probably unwise to try to assign relative determinations to correlated determining variables. Since in general determination is a complex thing, we do not lose much by failing to answer the question'.

Discriminant analysis is a special case of multiple regression. That fact is not widely known, because the theory of discriminant analysis was worked out before its relation to regression analysis was recognized. We take samples from two different populations (which might, for example, be two species), and measure various variates x on the individuals in the samples. The choice of what xs to measure is entirely ours. We know which individuals belong to which population. We now wish to take future individuals and assign them to one or other population, on the evidence of the xs. That is, we ask what is the linear combination of the xs that best discriminates between the two populations. Suppose we set up a dummy variate y, which takes values 0 for all individuals of one population and 1 for the other. (Any other pair of numbers would do as well as 0 and 1; it is the difference that is important.) Then the discriminant function is the multiple regression of y on the xs, when all the data are grouped together in one block. In fact, we are using the xs to predict a value 0 or 1 for each future individual. Here, the distribution of y itself is clearly not a Normal one, but theory shows that if the xs are Normally distributed, the y-remainders will be Normal, so that the usual significance tests are valid. (As mentioned above, usually in regressions the xs can have any distribution they like, provided that the y-residuals are Normal; in discriminant analysis, the xs are taken as Normal, just to ensure that the y-residuals shall be Normal.) By actually using this dummy y-variate in a multiple-regression program, we avoid the need to write a special program for discriminant analysis. There can be no guarantee that the function which best discriminates between two populations is also the best to discriminate either of the two from some third population. Therefore, although there exist techniques for discriminating between more than two populations simultaneously, they are not always very satisfactory.

In discriminant analysis, we already know to which group (population) each individual in the sample belongs, and we use the discriminant function to assign subsequent individuals to those groups. However, there also exist several methods of sorting the individuals in a sample into groups, purely by looking at the various measurements x made on those individuals. The groups are not defined in advance; instead, the computer impartially sorts the sample into groups of similar individuals. The question is, what does 'similar' mean? It can be shown that any desired grouping could be achieved, by adopting an appropriate definition of similarity. Methods of sorting must therefore be subjective, but they can still be useful for some defined purpose. For example, taxonomic classification is, to some extent, subjective, but it is still very useful.

The idea of regression is closely connected with that of correlation. Correlation, like regression, considers the *linear* relation between two variates, for example x and x^2 are not perfectly correlated. As we have seen, regression is used to predict y from x, so that y and x are not on an equal footing. The greater the correlation between x and y, the better the prediction will be. The correlation coefficient r measures the degree of linear co-relation between x and y, regarded as equal partners, and the regression of y on x tells us how much to expect y to change (because of the co-relation) in response to any given change in x. Although the regression lines of y on x, and of x on y, are not identical, the degree of predictability is the same in each case — in fact, either regression absorbs a fraction r^2 of the original sum of squares. A correlation always lies between -1 and $+1$, whereas a regression coefficient may take any value. Correlation coefficients used to be very important in statistical practice, but nowadays we usually think in terms of regression, which emphasizes the predictive aspect. Nevertheless, correlation coefficients are far from dead. For example, they are important in the theory of selection. Suppose we wish to select individuals for some desirable trait y, but we cannot measure y directly, and so have to make do with a correlated variate x. Then unless the correlation between x and y is perfect ($r = +1$ or -1), there will be errors of selection, and the more stringent the selection, the greater the frequency of mistakes. For example, if $r = 0.6$ and we select the 5 per cent of individuals who have the largest values of x, 31 per cent of those selected individuals would also have appeared in a selection for the top 5 per cent of ys: but if we select the top $\frac{1}{2}$ per cent of xs, only 15 per cent of the selected individuals would also have appeared in a selection for the top $\frac{1}{2}$ per cent of ys. (So university examinations, which assess innate ability by criteria which are imperfectly correlated with that ability, cannot be altogether accurate.) On the other hand, even if the correlation is very weak, mild selection for x can considerably increase the proportion of desirable ys.

Sometimes we wish to describe the correlations between many variates, without using them to predict some y-variate by regression. If there are more than about six variates, we are faced with a mass of correlation coefficients. For example, ten variates have forty five correlations between them. We cannot, unaided, grasp the pattern underlying so many individual correlations. Principal component analysis attempts to summarize the set of correlations. This paragraph does not describe the analysis in detail, but merely indicates what it is about. A principal component is an additive combination $a_1 x_1 + a_2 x_2 + \ldots + a_n x_n$ of the n original variates, with coefficients $a_1, a_2, \ldots a_n$ chosen so that $a_i a_j$ shall equal, as nearly as possible, the correlation r_{ij} between the ith and jth variates. The agreement cannot be perfect, because there are only n as being used to approximate $\frac{1}{2}n(n-1)$ rs. The first principal component is chosen to make the agreement as good as possible. Then a second principal component $b_1 x_1 + b_2 x_2 + \ldots + b_n x_n$ is chosen so that $b_i b_j$ shall approximate, as closely as possible, the remainders ($r_{ij} - a_i a_j$); and so on until a set of n principal components has been calculated, which together will reproduce perfectly the observed set of correlations. However, it is often found that the first two or three principal components suffice to summarize (near enough) the observed set of correlations, and therefore enable us to visualize how the variates 'hang together'. For example, suppose we have a set of measurements on beef carcasses. One principal component which represents a measure of 'over-all size', and a second component which apparently represents 'degree of fatness', can reproduce rather well — but not perfectly — the whole pattern of correlation between the several measurements. So, instead of having to consider hundreds of individual correlations, a cattle breeder need think only of those two principal components. It is tempting to suppose that those components measure some underlying biological process. Indeed, the very fact that it is possible to reduce a whole pattern of correlations to two components indicates that the original variates must be interconnected biologically — a conclusion that will surprise nobody. But the components are additive linear combinations of the variates, and it is most unlikely that the biological processes which give rise to the variates act in an additive linear fashion. So the components tell us nothing in detail about the underlying biology, but they do help us to visualize how the variates are connected. Factor analysis is closely related to principal component analysis. A given number of 'factors' will summarize a pattern of correlations rather better than the same number of principal components. But the actual values of the factors vary according to the number of factors used in the analysis. If I choose two factors, and you opt for three, your first two factors will differ from mine. No such difficulty arises with principal components. We can, of course, analyse a set of correlations for one factor, then for two, and so on until we have enough factors to give a satisfactory approximation to the whole set of correlations. But many people are suspicious of an analysis whose result depends, to some extent, on a rather arbitrary cut-off imposed by the statistician himself. They prefer the more objective, if rather less efficient, principal components. Actually, the two methods usually give very similar results. The major difficulties with either method are the lack of adequate significance tests (mathematical difficulties have so far prevented the development of an adequate theory) and the very questionable assumptions of additivity and linearity (Chap. 4).

In summary, nearly all bread-and-butter statistical methods can, if necessary, be reduced to eqn (3.5). Therefore, nearly all bread-and-butter statistical methods are versions of regression analysis. In biology, we take samples to find out how to predict unknown values of y in the population at large (Chap. 1). Therefore, regression analysis, which predicts y from xs, is usually far more important than functional relations, correlations, principal components, or factor analysis. Prediction is one thing, but determination and causality are quite another.

Regression, Correlation, and Determination

Examples 3

(1) A bacterial population was grown in a chemostat, starting from a few dozen cells. Successive samples gave the following counts per cm^3 of medium.

Time from start (minutes)	20	40	60	90	120	180	240	300	360	420
Bacterial count	47	62	73	103	220	537	1580	4500	9200	12800

Regress (a) the bacterial count, (b) the logarithm of the count, on time. Plot both (a) and (b) against time and draw in the regression lines. Which regression represents the growth best? Does it represent it satisfactorily?

(2) Humming birds were captured and weighed at various places on their migration route from Louisiana to Mexico.

Category 1 Adult Males		Category 2 Adult Females		Category 3 Juveniles	
Distance flown (miles)	Body weight (g)	Distance flown (miles)	Body weight (g)	Distance flown (miles)	Body weight (g)
450	2·8	450	2·9	260	4·1
450	3·2	260	3·4	260	3·7
450	2·8	260	2·9	260	4·3
260	3·0	70	4·1	70	5·0
260	3·7	70	4·1	70	4·2
70	4·2	70	3·6	70	4·3
70	3·8	70	4·0	70	4·8
70	3·7	70	3·8	70	5·3
720	1·9	720	2·5	720	2·8
720	2·3	720	2·2	720	1·9
		720	2·0		

Both distances and body weights are subject to errors of measurement. Calculate the regressions of body weight on distance and vice versa, in the three categories. If any of the categories may be combined, do so. What is the predicted weight of an adult humming bird after it has flown (a) 500 miles, (b) 2000 miles? What is the predicted distance flown by a juvenile bird weighing 2·0 gm?

(3) The regression of y on x is estimated from two separate blocks of data. The residual variance of y is the same in each block.
(a) What is the formula for the regression coefficient in block 1, and what is its variance?
(b) If we want to take the weighted average of the two estimates of b, what weights should we use?

(c) Therefore, what is the formula for the combined estimate of b? Now consider the same question, but dealing with the block means of y, instead of the regression b.

(4) Repeat Example 2 (Chap. 2) by multiple regression on dummy variates, grouping all the data together into one block. The simplest method is that described in the text, i.e. create one dummy variate for each lot of pigs (cf. breed of cows) and then use eqn (3.2) which contains no intercept. Multiple regression programs commonly use eqn (3.5) which includes an intercept a. There is then a technical difficulty; if we use a dummy variate for each lot of pigs, we shall be fitting *four* parameters, namely a, b_1, b_2, and b_3 to *three* lots of pigs. One of the parameters must be superfluous; it is a special case of 'linear dependence', discussed in Chapter 4. The difficulty is avoided by completely discarding any one of the three dummy variates. The analysis then appears lop-sided, but as we shall see, the answer comes out the same. This minor technical difficulty does not arise in an ordinary multiple regression, but only when the xs are dummy variates. So use two dummy variates — one to indicate whether an animal is Large White or not, and one for Landrace. Include the data for the Large White x Landrace cross (for which both the dummy xs will take zero values), but omit the aberrant value 4·37. When you have found the regression equation of growth rate on the two dummy variates, insert the appropriate values of x into it to find the expected growth rates of all three lots of pigs, and compare the answers with the average growth rates. What would be wrong with using a single dummy variate which takes values $x = 0$ for Large White, $x = 1$ for Landrace, and $x = 2$ for Large White x Landrace?

(5) The numbers of storks' nests counted in Jingistan, and the numbers of babies born, were as follows.

Year	Nests	Babies
1910	418	12 312
1911	422	12 208
1912	440	12 857
1913	440	12 819
1914	442	13 204
1915	454	13 670
1916	471	13 538
1917	473	14 111
1918	488	14 364
1919	495	14 437
1920	522	14 503
1921	518	14 866
1922	525	15 376

Regression, Correlation, and Determination

Show that the number of babies may be predicted from the number of storks' nests, but that after the calendar year has been included as an x-variate, the number of nests gives no extra prediction of the number of babies.

(6) Venetian cats steal fish and carry fleas in the following quantities:

Fish stolen in one year	Number of fleas on cat	Weight of cat (kg)
417	3	2·7
630	9	3·0
734	253	2·4
626	9	3·0
639	26	3·2
456	66	1·5
713	2	4·0
957	269	2·6

Show that the following are true.
(a) Cats which carry most fleas tend to steal most fish. Do the data prove that cats steal a lot of fish because they have a lot of fleas, or that they have a lot of fleas because they steal a lot of fish?
(b) The cat's weight cannot be predicted from the number of fish, or from the number of fleas, but
(c) the cat's weight can be predicted from the number of fish and the number of fleas in combination.

(7) The following table shows subjective scores of the suitability, as holiday areas, of a number of waterfront sites. At each site, the angle of slope x (degrees) was measured at three successive distances from the water.

Score y	x_1	x_2	x_3
3	30	10	0
2	25	25	0
1·5	15	15	15
3	25	15	15
3	30	30	10
4	50	35	0
2	20	0	0
5	30	30	30
4	35	35	35
2	20	10	20
5	40	40	40
3	10	10	10

Construct new variates $x_1 + x_3, x_1 - x_3, x_1 + x_2 + x_3$, and $(x_1 + x_2 + x_3)/3$.

(a) Regress y on all combinations of x_1, x_2, and x_3 to see which is best

(b) Show that the orders of preference of x_1, x_2, x_3 when 'building up' and 'stripping down' are different.

(c) Show that regression on $x_1 + x_3$ and $x_1 - x_3$ together is equivalent to regression on x_1 and x_3 together. Show, from the regression equation, that that must always be so.

(d) Show that in this case, $x_1 - x_3$ gives no extra prediction of the score after $x_1 + x_3$ has been included in the regression.

(e) Compare the single regressions of y on $x_1 + x_2 + x_3$ and $(x_1 + x_2 + x_3)/3$, and show that either gives as good prediction, in this case, as x_1, x_2, and x_3 together.

(8) Repeat Example 5 (Chap. 2) by multiple regression on dummy variates. Use one dummy variate to indicate Australian or not, one to indicate British or not, one to indicate male or not. Proceed as follows.

(a) Sort the data into cells, and do a one-way between-cells analysis of variance, to get a total 'between-cells' sum of squares and a 'remainder' sum of squares.

(b) Multiple regression on the first two dummies absorbs 'sum of squares for nationalities, ignoring sex'.

(c) Regression on the third dummy absorbs 'sum of squares for sex, ignoring nationalities'.

(d) Multiple regression on all three dummies absorbs 'sum of squares for nationalities and sex'.

(e) Subtract 'sum of squares for nationalities and sex' from total 'between-cells' sum of squares to get 'interactions' sum of squares.

(f) Subtract 'sum of squares for nationalities, ignoring sex' from 'sum of squares for nationalities and sex' to get 'extra sum of squares for sex, given nationalities'.

(g) Subtract 'sum of squares for sex, ignoring nationalities' from 'sum of squares for nationalities and sex' to get 'sum of squares for nationalities, given sex'.

Compare with the previous two-way analysis and with the least-squares theory of Chapter 1.

4 | ADDITIVITY AND LINEARITY

B E F O R E we can do any statistical analysis, we must (consciously or unconsciously) have a model. A model is an equation of the type

$$y_i = F_i + \text{remainder},$$

on which the analysis is based. For example, in Chapter 2 we had

$$y_{ij} = m + a_i + b_j + \text{interaction} + \text{remainder} \qquad (4.1)$$

for a two-way table, and, in Chapter 3,

$$y_i = a + bx_i + \text{remainder} \qquad (4.2)$$

for a single regression. The method of analysis also depends on the distribution of the residuals. Until now, we have used the method of least squares. For example, in eqn (4.2) we minimize the sum of squares $\Sigma(y_i - a - bx_i)^2/V_i$, where V_i is the variance of the residual of y_i. Before we can do the analysis, we must know (or postulate) V_i. Very often, we can assume that it is the same for every y_i, in which case we need only minimize the unweighted sum of squares $\Sigma(y_i - a - bx_i)^2$. If we suppose that V_i varies, we must minimize the weighted sum of squares $\Sigma w_i(y_i - a - bx_i)^2$, taking w_i to be $1/V_i$. In Chapter 7, we shall see that the method of least squares is a particular case of 'maximum likelihood'. Sometimes, it is necessary to abandon least squares, and use likelihood directly. But, in any case, once the model nas been decided on, and once the distribution of residuals has been determined, there can be only one correct method of analysis to answer any given biological question. It is true that the same analysis may be calculated in different ways, but the results will be the same. Given the model, and the distribution of the remainders, there is no room for 'we might try this method of analysis, or perhaps that one instead'. So, if two statisticians hand out contradictory advice, it means that (a) they have not understood the biological situation or the questions to be asked, (b) they are really saying the same thing in different ways, or (c) they think that different models, or different remainder distributions, are appropriate.

All the common statistical methods depend on additive models. Eqn (4.2) contains two addition signs, and eqn (4.1) has four. There is usually no reason why the underlying biological processes should be additive, but, as we shall see, additive models are usually good enough in practice. We can most easily think about a situation when it is additive; and additive models demand relatively simple calculations and theory. The everyday use of orthodox (additive) methods was laborious before the invention of desk calculators. Now that we have computers, orthodox analyses can be done very easily, and we could certainly try to develop more penetrating, non-additive methods. But, at present, computers are used mainly to proliferate additive statistical analyses. That is due, in part, to conservatism but, very largely, it is because additive methods are quite satisfactory for most purposes.

Since the analysis depends on an additive model, we must be reasonably confident that the data do, at least approximately, conform to that model. If not, it may be advisable to transform the scale of measurement until they do (Chap. 5). It is usually a matter of experience and judgement to decide whether a given set of data conform well enough to an additive model, but, sometimes, the question can be tested statistically. For example, in a multiple regression of y on x_1 and x_2, we can construct an additional variate $x_3 = x_1 \times x_2$. If the extra regression on x_3 is significant, it means that the data do not completely satisfy the additive regression model

$$y = a + b_1 x_1 + b_2 x_2.$$

Tukey (1949) developed the corresponding test for orthogonal two-way tables. It is true that these tests only look for one particular pattern of non-additivity, but they can usually indicate the existence of serious departures from additivity, even if the actual pattern is different.

We shall see in Chapter 6 that significance tests assume the remainders to be Normally distributed, and, in Chapter 7, that the method of least squares is most easily justified by the same assumption. There is a very close connection between additivity and Normality. If a quantity y is the additive sum of many independent contributions, the Central Limit Theorem tells us that (under very weak conditions which are nearly always fulfilled) y will be Normally distributed. That theorem would not be true if, instead, y were (say) the multiplicative product of many independent contributions. Conversely, if y_1 and y_2 are Normally

Additivity and Linearity

distributed, then $y_1 + y_2$ and $y_1 - y_2$ also are Normally distributed, but other non-additive combinations of y_1 and y_2 are not.

In practice, then, we work as follows. We make sure that it is reasonable to suppose that, on the chosen scale of measurement, the effects of treatment will be roughly additive. If not, we transform the scale of measurement. We then use the argument developed in Chapter 5 that, if the treatment effects are additive, the relatively small remainders are likely to be Normally distributed. (It does not follow that the remainder variance V_i will necessarily be homogeneous.) Certainly, there are tests to see if the remainders are really Normal, but those tests are not often applied, firstly, because they require a large body of data to distinguish any moderate departure from Normality, and then because a large body of data will rarely conform exactly to the Normal distribution. As we shall see in the next paragraph, that does not matter. In practice, additive models give satisfactory results, provided that we do not trust them implicitly. The danger is to assume that, because an additive model fits the data, the underlying biological processes must themselves act additively. Chapter 10 illustrates the unfortunate consequences of such an assumption.

We may well ask, 'Is it not dangerous to use methods, based on the assumption of Normally distributed remainders, without checking that assumption carefully in every case?' We rely heavily on the fact that many statistical methods are 'robust', that is, they do not go seriously wrong in the face of reasonable departures from Normality. Means, regressions, and t-tests are reliable, provided that the distribution of y remainders is unimodal (i.e. has only one peak or hump) and is not badly skew. However, variances are much more sensitive. Usually this does not matter, because we use variances merely to calculate standard errors, that is, to assess the accuracy of what concerns us most, namely, the means or regressions. But sometimes the variances are analysed for their own sake. It is then easy, for several reasons, to get quite misleading results.

Suppose we have a sum of squares Σy^2, with n degrees of freedom. The ys might, for example, be original observations, but usually they will be residuals. In that case, the number of degrees of freedom will be less than the number of ys in the sum of squares. Suppose that the ys are Normally distributed, with a true (population) mean of zero and variance V. Then $\Sigma y^2 /V$ has a χ^2 distribution with n degrees of freedom That is, if we take many such sums of squares Σy^2, the various values of $\Sigma y^2 /V$ will follow the χ^2 distribution, because that is how the χ^2

distribution is defined. When we use χ^2 in practice, it is usually to analyse data which are whole-number counts. That is an approximate use of χ^2; the calculated values of χ^2 conform only approximately to the true χ^2 distribution, because the residuals used to calculate χ^2 are only approximately Normal. Thus, we need to obey the rules which ensure that the approximation shall be a good one (Chap. 6). However, χ^2 is basically the distribution of sums of squares of Normally distributed ys whose mean is zero. So, if we take numerous sets of observations, and work out Σy^2 for each set, the χ^2 distribution will tell us how much variation in $\Sigma y^2/V$ to expect. We can then deduce the variation in Σy^2 itself.

The average, or expected, value of χ^2 is always n, its number of degrees of freedom. For, if Σy^2 is a sum of squares with n degrees of freedom, the mean square $\Sigma y^2/n$ is an estimate of the population variance V. $\Sigma y^2/n$ on average equals V, and so χ^2, i.e. $\Sigma y^2/V$, on average equals n. If we look at a table of χ^2, we see that the value of χ^2 equals the number of degrees of freedom, somewhere near the middle of the probability distribution. Suppose, for example, that $n = 30$. The average value of χ^2 will be 30, but the table of χ^2 gives 18·493 for the 95 per cent probability point, and 43·773 for the 5 per cent point. (These two values are not symmetrical about the mean 30, since the χ^2 distribution is skew.) So, the 95 per cent and 5 per cent points of $\chi^2/30$ are 18·493/30 and 43·773/30, i.e. 0·62 and 1·46. That is, of a series of mean squares (each with 30 degrees of freedom) intended to estimate a variance V, 5 per cent will come out less than $0·62V$, and another 5 per cent will be more than $1·46V$, and so the estimate of V will often be very inaccurate. Now, if we found that an estimate of a mean had a standard error of 20 per cent, we should think that estimate very inaccurate, or even worthless in many cases, yet that is the kind of accuracy that must be expected from mean squares. If we are interested in the size of the variance for its own sake, a mean square with even as many as 30 degrees of freedom may easily give a very inaccurate estimate. (Usually, of course, we calculate a mean square merely in order to assess the accuracy of a mean or regression coefficient. The published tables of t then make automatic allowance for the inaccuracy of the mean square as an estimate of V.) With fewer degrees of freedom, estimates of variance are even worse. That is the first intrinsic difficulty in analysing variances *per se*. The second is that (as mentioned above) estimates of variance are not robust, i.e. departures from Normality tend to make them even more inaccurate. For instance, one aberrant value in a sample will not change the mean too much, but will seriously distort the mean square (Example 2, Chap. 2). Thirdly, when analysing variances in their own right, we may want to estimate, not the variances themselves, but the 'components of variance'. These components have nothing to do with the 'principal components' of a set of correlations, mentioned in Chapter 3. I shall not discuss components of variance in detail here; they are not used in everyday statistical practice, and it is doubtful if they are very helpful anyway. Chapter 10 discusses their use in genetics. Suffice it to say, that after an analysis of variance has split the total sum of squares into two or more sums of squares, the corresponding mean squares may (if desired) themselves be interpreted as the sums of 'components' which purport to represent various kinds of biological variability. But there are serious difficulties. Firstly, the components are rather different for a 'fixed-effects' model and for a 'random-effects' model. We have already met that distinction in Chapter 2. A fixed-effects model is concerned only with the particular treatments being analysed, whereas a random-effects model regards the treatments as a random sample from some population of possible treatments. It is often very difficult to decide whether a fixed- or random-effects model is most appropriate to a given case, and some people deny that the distinction has any merit at all. It is fortunate, therefore, that the distinction between fixed and random effects actually makes little difference to the answer in practice. Secondly, the components are found by subtracting one mean square from another. But if one mean square may estimate the true value inaccurately, the difference of two mean squares will be even less reliable; indeed, components of variance sometimes come out negative, which they should not. Thirdly, estimates of components of variance depend very critically on the assumption of additivity. Even the experts can go badly wrong when trying to interpret variances *per se*. That will not, perhaps, surprise those people who have much experience of experts. None of these difficulties arise when variances are used in the usual way to assess the accuracy of means or regressions.

In Chapter 2, we observed that to describe a whole distribution, both the mean and the variance (or alternatively, the standard deviation) must be quoted. Occasionally, then, we want to analyse the variance of y in much the same way as we analyse its mean, but without getting involved in the complexities of 'components of variance'. In plant breeding, for example, reliability of yield is as important as average size of yield. A variety may be chosen because its performance does not vary much from year to year, or from place to place. We may use a mean square to estimate the variability of a variety, just as we use the mean to estimate its yield. Since the distribution of χ^2 is very skew, it is best to apply a transform, and analyse log (mean square). For example, Bartlett's test examines the homogeneity of a set of mean squares, by comparing their logarithms. We still cannot escape from the fact that variances are not robust; Bartlett's test is very sensitive to departures from Normality. It is equally possible to regress log (mean square of y) on some concomitant variate x, to see if x can predict the variability of y. Example 1 of this chapter considers the special case where x is, in fact, $\bar{y}$. Instead of log (mean square), the cube root $\sqrt[3]{}$ (mean square) is equally satisfactory.

Additive models, e.g. eqn (4.2), quite naturally lead to the use of regression methods, since eqn (4.2) *is* the basic regression equation. It assumes that the relation between y and x is a straight line, but the data may not agree. Just as, earlier in this chapter, it was possible to test for non-additivity by an extra regression on $x_1 \times x_2$, so it is possible to test for non-linearity by the extra regression on x^2. It does not follow that, if the test detects some curvature, that curvature is necessarily quadratic. If the test detects some serious non-linearity, the only sure way to see what kind of curvature is actually involved is to plot y against x, graphically. If the curvature is slight, however, it may be good enough to ignore it, and say 'the linear regression gives predictions which, although not perfect, are good enough for present purposes'. Otherwise, there are several ways of dealing with non-linearity. Examination of the plot of y against x often suggests that some transformation of y or x will convert the relation to a straight line. A transformation of y will not only straighten the relation between y and x, but will alter the structure of the y-remainders, which is sometimes desirable (Chap. 5). On the other hand, a transformation of x will leave the y-residuals unaltered in structure (Example 3, Chapter 5).

It is best to convert the situation to a straight line if possible, partly because we can then use linear regression methods, and partly because it is easier to think in terms of linearity. But another way of dealing with curvature is to use a polynomial regression. This is the multiple regression of y on $x, x^2, x^3 \ldots$ to as many terms as may be necessary to fit the observed relation between y and x. Two practical points arise. Firstly, the values of $x, x^2, x^3 \ldots$ are themselves highly correlated. In order to estimate the multiple-regression coefficients accurately, it is often desirable to use $(x - \bar{x}), (x - \bar{x})^2, (x - \bar{x})^3 \ldots$ instead (Healy

51

Additivity and Linearity

1963). If the polynomial goes beyond $(x - \bar{x})^5$, even more sophisticated manipulation may be advisable. When the values of x are equally spaced along the x-axis, the difficulty may be avoided by using orthogonal polynomials (Fisher and Yates 1953). Secondly, it sometimes happens that, in a polynomial, some power of x (less than the highest) contributes insignificantly to the regression, so that it could apparently be omitted without loss. That is not a useful thing to do, partly because of notions of completeness (dislike of leaving a 'hole' in the middle of a polynomial), but partly because the consequent adjustment of the remaining terms in the regression might distort the prediction of y at some point in the range of x. It is, of course, very dangerous to extrapolate any empirical prediction formula outside the range of values of x and y from which it was estimated, unless there is some other justification, perhaps theoretical, for so doing. Polynomials are useful but inelegant. Many terms may have to be included before a polynomial can predict the values of y as well as can some simple algebraic function of x, such as (for example) $x \log x$. Many people prefer to use such algebraic functions wherever possible, reserving polynomials as a last resort — as a sledgehammer which can, if necessary, crack any nut. The choice of appropriate functions of x is discussed in Chapter 13. But, sometimes, no simple transform to linearity is possible. For example, we might decide to fit the relation

$$y = a - be^{-kx} + \text{remainder}$$

to a set of data. That relation cannot be transformed to a linear regression from which the values of a, b, and k could be estimated. We must resort to a third method of dealing with curvature, i.e. non-linear regression. The principle is just the same as in ordinary regression. We find the values of a, b, and k which minimize the 'remainder' sum of squares, $\Sigma(y_i - a + be^{-kx})^2$; but the calculation can no longer be done in one stage, it is necessary to find a, b, and k in several steps, by trial and error. There are several possible methods of calculation. No one method is best in all cases, indeed, if the wrong method is chosen in any given case, it is quite possible to go on calculating *ad infinitum*, without ever converging on the right values of a, b, and k. Special computer programs exist to do the job, but it is quite often good enough to use an ordinary regression program. In this case, we might choose a series of trial values of k, and find the values of a and b corresponding to each value of k by regression of y on e^{-kx}. We then choose the value of k which gives the best prediction of y (Example 2, Chap. 13).

Suppose we wish to estimate a regression, and can ourselves choose the values of x, before we measure the corresponding ys. The most accurate estimate of b is obtained by making half the xs as large as possible, and the other half as small as possible. There are two ways of seeing this. Firstly, the regression line is 'anchored' better by extreme values than by values near the centre of the graph. Secondly, the variance of b is estimated by $s^2/\Sigma(x_i - \bar{x})^2$ (Chap. 3). To make that variance small, $\Sigma(x_i - \bar{x})^2$ should be large, i.e. the values of $(x_i - \bar{x})^2$ must all be as large as possible. If it were absolutely certain that the regression must be linear, it would be best to choose the xs in that way. But then the curvature of the regression could not be examined, and so it is usually advisable to include some intermediate values of x. If a gap is left in the range of values of x, predictions of y in the middle of that gap may be very inaccurate.

If we are interested in two variates x_1 and x_2, we may find that the difference $x_1 - x_2$ is even more interesting. For example, the male and female flowers of a maize plant mature at different times, so that the plant cannot fertilize itself. If x_1 and x_2 are the times of male and female flowering, the difference $x_1 - x_2$ is genetically important. We wish to predict some variate y from the xs. It might seem reasonable to write $x_3 = x_1 - x_2$, and regress y on x_1, x_2, and x_3; that will not work. The three x-variates are linearly dependent, and any one of them may be omitted without loss. It is easy to see why. If

$$y = a + b_1 x_1 + b_2 x_2 + b_3 x_3 + \text{remainder},$$

then $\qquad y = a + b_1 x_1 + b_2 x_2 + b_3(x_1 - x_2) + \text{remainder},$

i.e. $\qquad y = a + (b_1 + b_3)x_1 + (b_2 - b_3)x_2 + \text{remainder}.$

The regression on x_1, x_2, and x_3 is equivalent to regression on x_1 and x_2 only. Any x-variate which is a linear combination of previous x-variates is superfluous. A multiple regression program should recognize and comment on such a situation. However, sometimes a set of x-variates are almost, but not quite, linearly dependent. For example, that may happen if (as mentioned above) we regress y on $x, x^2, x^3 \ldots$ The analysis then becomes very unreliable; small errors in the values of x may seriously affect the regression coefficients. The standard errors of (some of) the regression coefficients will then be very large, and the situation may be recognized in that way. Because of the way it does its arithmetic, a computer may fail to recognize that a set of x-variates are linearly dependent, in which case the results will show the same

Additivity and Linearity

warning signals (very large standard errors) as if the xs were *almost* linearly dependent.

Examples 4

(1) *Coefficient of variation.* As mentioned in Chapter 5, the variance of x often increases as the mean increases. If m_1 exceeds m_2, nobody will be surprised if the corresponding V_1 also exceeds V_2. Can we compare the intrinsic variability of two populations? Suppose the two means are sharply different, so that the ranges of x in the two populations do not overlap. Then it is possible to find a transformation of the scale of x, to make V_1/V_2 take any value we like (Chap. 5). However, if the two means are nearly equal, so that one population overlaps the other at both ends, the first population will be more variable than the second on any scale of measurement. So we cannot say that one population is intrinsically more variable than another, unless the ranges of x overlap, or unless a particular scale of measurement is specified. The 'coefficient of variation', equal to the standard deviation divided by $\bar{x}$, is a dimensionless measure of variability, that is, if we change the units of measurement (say from inches to centimetres) the coefficient of variation remains unaltered. We cannot use the coefficient to compare the intrinsic variabilities of two populations with sharply different means, unless we are sure that (other things being equal), as m changes, V will remain proportional to m^2 (which it must if the coefficient of variation is not to change as m changes). In practice, it is found that, in a set of similar samples with different means, s^2 is proportional to $\bar{x}^b$, where b is some constant. Usually, b does not equal 2, and so the 'coefficient of variation' will change as m changes, but $\log s^2$ may be predicted by linear regression on $\log \bar{x}$ (Southwood 1966).

(2) The daily growth (increase in stem length) of a maize plant was measured on eight consecutive days, together with sunshine and rainfall.

Growth (cm)	Hours of sunshine	Rain (in)
2·1	2·4	0·66
2·4	6·5	0·14
3·2	7·6	0·00
2·9	7·5	0·02
3·0	7·1	0·07
2·8	4·4	0·40
2·6	5·9	0·22
2·6	7·0	0·08

Examine the regression of growth on sunshine and rain. In this case, the sunshine and rain records are very highly correlated. They are nearly, but not quite, linearly dependent. Both give equally good prediction of growth, and the multiple regression of growth on sunshine and rain is completely erratic. Actually, the growth rate is *determined* neither by sunshine nor by rain, but by a third correlated variable, namely temperature.

(3) Example 4 (Chap. 1) states that if we divide a sum of squares by its 'degrees of freedom', we get a mean square which estimates the population variance V. It can be shown, theoretically, that this is always true if we use an additive model, but need not be true if the model is not additive.

5 | TRANSFORMATIONS

THERE is usually no reason why we should insist on analysing data on their original scale of measurement. If we are dealing with (say) numbers of animals, we can think just as well in terms of log N as of N itself. It is true that for some strictly practical things, e.g. pest numbers, we are directly concerned with numbers and not with the square roots of numbers. But, even then, it may be technically best to do the statistical analysis on a transformed scale, and finally change the answer back to the original scale.

There are three reasons for using transformations:

(1) to make the remainder variances uniform,
(2) to make the distribution of errors Normal,
(3) to make the effects of treatments additive.

(1) Suppose we wish to compare the means of several blocks of data in a one-way analysis of variance. The usual analysis assumes that the remainder variance of single observations is the same in every block. (That does not imply that the block *means* must all have the same accuracy, unless the number of observations per block is the same in every block.) Fortunately, the method of analysis is insensitive − or robust − to reasonable departures from that assumption. And since the remainder variance within any block is usually correlated with the block mean itself, we need not worry too much, provided that the block means all have the same order of magnitude, and provided that the data have all been collected (measured) by the same method in every block. But, if one block has mean 10 and another has mean 100 (i.e. there is an order of magnitude of difference between the blocks), it is unlikely that the remainder variance will be as great in the former block as in the latter. This, in theory at any rate, invalidates the usual analysis − although the disparity must be very great, before it makes any real difference to the biological answer obtained. One way of rectifying the trouble is to transform the scale of observation. Thus, for a Poisson distribution,

the variance of n equals the average value of n, and, hence, the variance of $\sqrt{n}$ is approximately independent of the level of size of n. Again, the Binomial distribution with proportion p has variance $p(1 - p)$, but the angular transformation gives almost uniform variance for all values of p between 0 and 1.

(2) If the distribution of remainders is not Normal, the analysis itself will be unaffected (unless the departure from Normality is so enormous that the analysis wastes most of the information contained in the sample — see Chapter 7), but significance tests based on the Normal distribution will be upset. Significance tests of differences between *means* are not greatly affected unless the departure from Normality is extreme, but tests on *variances* (e.g. variance-ratio and Bartlett's test) are much more sensitive. Transformations may be used to give Normality, e.g. the logarithmic transformation will, by definition, transform a log Normal distribution to a Normal one. However, those of us who deplore the automatic, unthinking application of significance tests will not be very upset if tests do give rather inaccurate answers.

(3) As pointed out in Chapter 4, nearly all statistical methods assume that treatments have additive effects; partly because the theory is then algebraically tractable, and partly because the calculations are then fairly straightforward. Suppose we are dealing with percentages (e.g., of a given sample of animals, so many are male). A treatment which converts 2 per cent into 3 per cent (i.e. adds 1 per cent) is unlikely to change 25 per cent into 26 per cent; more likely, it will increase 25 per cent to, perhaps, 28 per cent. Since percentages below 0 or above 100 are impossible, the original scale of percentages is tight at either end, but is relatively open in the middle. The angular transformation is then used to make the assumption (that treatments have additive effects) more reasonable. Similarly, if we are dealing with counts of animals, it is quite likely that some treatment which changes a count from 10 to 20, will be acting multiplicatively, and so change 100 to 200 rather than to 110. The logarithmic transformation then converts the situation to an additive one.

Of reasons (1), (2), and (3), the third is by far the most important. That is because difficulties (1) and (2) may be dealt with in other ways: (1) by using an analysis which is weighted to allow for the heterogeneity of variance (Chap. 1), and (2) by working out tests suitable for the

Transformations

particular kind of non-Normal distribution. But since the basic statistical methods assume additivity, we are forced to use scales of measurement which, at least approximately, make that assumption reasonable. However, reasons (1), (2), and (3) are interconnected, so that a transformation which deals with (3) will very likely satisfy (1) and (2) — but not necessarily vice versa. If the size of a treatment effect remains the same at all points on the scale of measurement, it is likely that the size of the relatively small remainders will also be uniform, i.e. that the remainder variance will be the same at all points of the scale. If there is reason to suspect serious heterogeneity of variance, the treatment effects may well be non-additive too. It is therefore more common to use a transformation than a weighted analysis to deal with heterogeneity of variance. If the treatment effects are additive, the relatively small residuals will tend to be additive too, and hence the distribution of remainders is likely to be approximately Normal (Chap. 4).

If the range of variation in the whole set of data is small, there may be no need to transform, even though the data are of a kind that would otherwise need transformation. For example, if we are dealing with percentages varying from 10 to 50, it would be advisable to apply the angular transform; but if the range of percentages is only 20 to 35, we should obtain almost precisely the same biological answer, whether we transformed or not. That is because a transformation, in effect, curves the scale of measurement, and, if the range of observations is small, only a short piece of the scale is used, and the curvature will have no serious effect.

The following are some commonly used transformations.

(a) *The angular (or arc sin $\sqrt{x}$).* This is applied to percentages lying strictly between 0 and 100 (or to fractions x between 0 and 1). As mentioned above, it has the effect of stretching the scale at each end, and so it is not suitable where the percentage can exceed 100, e.g., percentage increases in numbers (in such cases, we might, perhaps, consider using a logarithmic transformation, which stretches the scale at the bottom end). The angular transform is often applied as a matter of course to binomial data, e.g. 'of N animals, so many per cent are of this kind'. Although the angular transform can solve the problem of non-additive treatment effects, it takes no notice of the sample size N. An individual percentage, based on N observations, will be intrinsically more accurate if N is large than if N is small. Thus, if we are analysing a set of percentages; and if the number N, on which the individual percentages are based, is very variable, we may need to apply the angular transformation (to obtain additivity of treatment effects) and *then* use a weighted analysis (to allow for the fact that different observations, being based on radically different numbers, have different accuracies). In that case, the variance of each transformed percentage would be proportional to $1/N$; the appropriate weight would be $1/(\text{variance})$ (Chap. 1), and so the weight used would be simply N.

(b) *Square root.* This is appropriate to counts with a Poisson distribution. Its effect is to make the larger values less important compared with the smaller. For example, it converts the series 0, 1, 4 to 0, 1, 2. On the original scale, the difference between 0 and 4 is four times that between 0 and 1, whereas on the new scale, the corresponding difference is only twice as large. The greatest value (4) has become relatively less important.

(c) *The logarithmic transform.* This is usually applied to counts with an 'over-dispersed' distribution, such as the negative Binomial or Logarithmic. In the case of a truly negative Binomial distribution, there is a special *ad hoc* transformation which may be used, but it gives much the same answer as the simpler logarithmic transform. The logarithmic transform, like the square-root transform, serves to stretch out the bottom end of the scale, but the effect of the logarithmic is much more severe than that of the square root. To avoid trouble when $n = 0$, it is usual to analyse, not log n, but $\log(n + c)$, where c is some constant. Usually, c is arbitrarily chosen to be 1; the larger the value of c, the less severe is the effect of the transformation. Similarly, $\sqrt{(n + c)}$ (where c is a positive constant) is a less severe transform than $\sqrt{n}$. There are theories to prove that, for purpose (1), some value of c such as 3/8 is optimal, but such theories become trivial when it is recognized that the main point of transformations is for purpose (3). The logarithmic transform is often used successfully on counts of animal or plant populations, but there is no theoretical reason why it should always be the best in such cases (Chap. 11).

(d) *Probits and logits.* These are special-purpose transforms used to facilitate the analysis of biological assays.

Before the advent of computers, it was sometimes difficult to decide which transformation to use in any given case. Fortunately, we learn from experience that two transformations of approximately the same severity will give the same biological answer; indeed, in most cases, even a transform as severe as the logarithmic will give the same biological answer as does analysis of the untransformed data. (The severity of any given transformation may be judged by plotting the transformed scale

Transformations

against the original scale, over the range of values concerned in the analysis.) In cases where the answer obtained depends on which transform is used, we must either examine the data to see if some particular transform is most appropriate, or perhaps abandon the data as inadequate to answer the biological question satisfactorily. Nowadays, it is a simple matter to perform the same analysis with different transforms to check that the same biological answer is obtained. If the analysis on a logarithmic scale gives much the same answer as the analysis on the untransformed scale, it follows that analysis on any intermediate scale would also give that answer.

In Chapter 2 we discussed the presentation of numerical results. A special problem may arise when transformations have been used. Means, standard errors, etc. have been calculated on the transformed scale. It is often sufficient to quote the results entirely on the transformed scale, in which case no problem arises; but, sometimes, it is desirable to translate the results of an analysis, performed on the transformed scale, back to the original scale of measurement. That is easily done for means; for example, if we have analysed a set of original measurements y on the scale of $\log y$, we can quote the antilogarithm of the mean value of $\log y$. That antilogarithm will, in fact, be the *geometric* mean of y. The same considerations which prompted us to use the logarithmic transform also assure us that the geometric mean will, in this case, represent the values of y better than a straightforward arithmetic mean. But it is not possible to quote standard errors on the untransformed scale. Standard errors will be symmetrical about the mean on the transformed scale, but not on the original scale. The difficulty may be avoided in two ways. We may quote, on the original scale, asymmetric confidence limits (found by re-converting the symmetric confidence limits of the transformed scale; in the logarithmic case mentioned above, these limits would be quoted about the geometric mean of y). Alternatively, we can give two sets of results, one (with standard errors) on the transformed scale, and the corresponding set of means only (on the original scale). The reader can then judge both the significance (on the transformed scale) and the practical importance (on the original scale) of the results.

Transformations are also used *mathematically*, to convert a curvilinear relation to a linear one (Chap. 4). If often happens that some transform, chosen for mathematical reasons, is also suitable statistically; but there is no theoretical reason why that should be, except that linearity and additivity often occur together.

60

Examples 5

(1) Plot the following transforms of y, for $y = 0, 1, 2 \ldots 20$.

(a) $\sqrt{y}$,
(b) $\log (1 + y)$,
(c) $\sqrt[3]{y}$,
(d) $\exp(y)$,

and, for $y = 0, 5, 10 \ldots 100$,

(e) angular transform of y per cent.

Compare the effects and severities of these transforms. It is the *shape* of the transformation that matters, rather than the absolute size of the transformed values.

(2) **Repeat Example 2 (Chap. 2)** using logarithmic and square-root transforms. Convert means back to the original scale of measurement. Do these transformations affect the biological answer, in this case?

(3) The body lengths and skinned carcase weights of twelve rabbits were as follows.

Length (cm)	Carcase weight (g)
30	2453
25	1148
26	1406
35	3062
30	2292
32	2981
25	1358
28	1718
29	2138
23	1051
31	2054
30	1951

We want to predict carcase weights from body lengths. We might expect that carcase weight is proportional to length^3 (why?). Plot (a) carcase weight against length, (b) carcase weight against length^3, and (c) $\sqrt[3]{}$(carcase weight) against length. Is it better to use transformation (b) or (c) before doing a linear regression?

(4) An extreme case. Suppose that, of a sample of N animals, all are found to be female. Then the proportion p of males is estimated to be zero, and the variance of that estimate (i.e. $p(1 - p)/N$) is also zero. Thus, we seem to have arrived at the conclusion that the proportion of males in the population is estimated to be zero with standard error zero, i.e. there are no males at all in the population. However, the absence of

Transformations

males from the sample might be due to chance. No amount of transformation can help us here. Instead, we argue as follows. Suppose the true frequency of males is p. The probability that all animals in the sample are female is then $(1 - p)^N$. The '95 per cent confidence limit for p' is that value of p, which makes $(1 - p)^N$ equal to 0.05, any larger value of p would make the all-female sample very unlikely. Work out this confidence limit for $N = 10$ and $N = 100$.

(5) Suppose we are analysing the distribution of the number of tapeworms per wild deer. Quite often, there are some animals which have a lot of worms, but many which have none. The distribution may be so lop-sided, or even two-humped, i.e. frequency of zeros may be so great (in comparison with $1s$, $2s$, $3s$ . . .), that no transformation can reasonably deal with it. In that case, we may have to do separate analyses, the first on the ratio of deer without worms to deer with worms, and the second on the numbers of worms per infected deer. That is, the zero term is analysed separately. The two analyses will usually reinforce each other, telling the same biological story.

6 | SIGNIFICANCE TESTS

STATISTICAL analyses help the biologist to draw appropriate conclusions (and avoid inappropriate ones) from his data; but the biologist must still take responsibility for those conclusions. Significance tests are only an aid in judging the results of an analysis. The variance-ratio (or F-) test is not an integral part of the analysis of variance: it is a tool which can help us interpret the results of that analysis. Some people hope, by the automatic use of significance tests, to avoid personal responsibility for the biological interpretation. That hope is vain. The test says, '*Either* something improbable has happened *or* there is a real effect'. Purely by chance, the result will be significant at the 5 per cent level once every twenty times; so the test cannot *prove* that there is a real effect. Even if the result of the test is not significant, it does not follow that there is no real effect. All that the test can do, is to assess the chance of obtaining the data, in the absence of the effect in question. Significance tests can help in the interpretation of data, but so can commonsense, a knowledge of biology, and an intimate acquaintance with the data. Consider, for example, the rejection of outliers. A set of data sometimes contains an outlying value, considerably different from the other values. The outlying value might be genuine, or it might be spurious, in which case it ought to be rejected. So we have to decide if an egregious value may be regarded as part of the sample, or whether it is wrong. Inclusion of an erroneous outlier can bias the answer, and (especially) inflate the variance. Sometimes we refer back to the original source of measurement, and sometimes the observation is biological nonsense; but, otherwise, the question is best settled by commonsense. A border-line case will not make much difference to the answer, whether it is included or rejected. True, there exist special tests to detect outliers, but if applied sufficiently enthusiastically, those tests could eliminate nearly all the observations in a sample. Particularly serious, is a slavish reliance on arbitrary levels of significance. There is nothing magic about 5 per cent and 1 per cent. Some people think that if a result is 'significant at 4 per cent probability' it must be accepted, but that if the probability is 6 per cent, the result must be ignored. But, in fact, both the 4 per cent and the 6 per cent merely assess the possibility that the result occurred by chance: the 6 per cent probability is rather less significant than the 4 per cent. As a general rule, if the significance is at this borderline level, further work is needed to establish the reality of the effect in question.

Commonly used are the t-, F- (or variance-ratio), and χ^2 tests. They all assume that the remainders are Normally distributed. If that assumption is wrong, the test will wrongly assess the significance probability. If the true distribution were known, it would be possible to adjust the test accordingly. The t-test, which compares *means*, is more robust, i.e. less sensitive to departures from Normality, than the F- and χ^2 tests, which are concerned with *variances*. We shall see that these three tests are interrelated, so that they cannot contradict each other. They can return only *one* answer to any given question. Non-parametric tests, on the other hand, avoid the assumption of a Normal (or any other) distribution of remainders. They do so by concentrating on some particular aspect of the data, which can be analysed distribution-free. For example, a non-parametric test may consider only the signs of the residuals, not their actual sizes. Non-parametric tests, therefore, tend to be rather less 'efficient' than the F-, t-, or χ^2 tests, when applied to Normally distributed remainders, because they ignore some of the information which those remainders can convey. In practice, however, some non-parametric tests compare very favourably with the orthodox tests, especially when the data are not truly Normally distributed. Sometimes, there are several non-parametric tests which may each be used to examine some given question (for instance, the difference of two means). Those tests will give rather different answers, because they concentrate on different aspects of the data. Some people try one test after another, in the 'hope' that one of them will achieve some arbitrary level of significance. Such people delude themselves: by insisting on arbitrary 5 per cent or 1 per cent levels, they betray a misunderstanding of the nature of a significance test.

The multiple-range tests show how the automatic use of significance tests can give misleading results. Suppose we wish to compare a set of 'treatment' means. We have already seen (Chap. 2) that if the 'treatments' mean square significantly exceeds the 'remainder' mean square, we may take some notice of unexpected differences revealed by inspection of the treatment means. Multiple-range tests try to identify the similarities and dissimilarities among a set of treatment means, allowing for the fact that numerous comparisons (not all independent, in the sense of Chapter 2) may be made between them. Although there are some technical objections to multiple-range tests, they are widely used, especially in North America. However, it is often the pattern of a set of 'treatment' means, rather than the exact difference between any pair of them, that is important. Multiple-range tests dissect the over-all biological pattern into a set of rather arbitrary discontinuities. Many people do not use those tests at all, but simply examine the whole set of 'treatment' means (with standard errors), bearing in mind their biological meaning. Multiple-range tests merely delay the time when we have to say, 'I think the results mean so-and-so'.

A value of t is always 'something, divided by its standard error'. The 'something' might be the difference between a mean and its theoretical value (often zero); or the difference between two means; or, perhaps, a comparison between regression coefficients. Strictly speaking, a calculated value of t should be compared with the printed table of values of t, only when the remainders are Normally distributed. But the t-test is robust, that is, it can tolerate reasonable departures from Normality. Here is another way of thinking about the t-test. Its denominator, a standard error, is calculated from a set of remainders, that is, from a set of comparisons among the sample values y. The standard error is, therefore, a kind of average of many comparisons. So the value of t is 'a comparison, divided by an average of many such comparisons'. When we use t to test a biological effect that does not in fact exist, the numerator and denominator of t should be about the same size, provided that we have calculated the standard error correctly. It is, of course, unlikely that they will be exactly the same size. The printed table of t tells us whether the calculated value could reasonably be obtained by chance. In practice, t must be at least 2 before it can be judged 'significant'. Two 'rough-and-ready' rules can save a lot of time. Suppose we wish to use t to compare two quantities whose remainder variances are V_1 and V_2, respectively. Assuming that the quantities are uncorrelated, the variance of their difference is $V_1 + V_2$, and so the standard error is $\sqrt{(V_1 + V_2)}$. If V_1 and V_2 are approximately equal, $\sqrt{(V_1 + V_2)}$ is approximately $\frac{3}{2}$ times either $\sqrt{V_1}$ or $\sqrt{V_2}$, that is, the standard error of the difference is about $\frac{3}{2}$ times the standard error of either of the two original quantities. However, if V_1 is much bigger than V_2, $\sqrt{(V_1 + V_2)}$ is little bigger than $\sqrt{V_1}$, and so the standard error of the difference is about the same as the standard error of the least accurate of the original quantities. These rules often make it unnecessary to actually calculate values of t, except in borderline cases; and even in borderline cases, the exact level of significance is not very important.

Since t is 'a comparison, divided by its standard error', it follows that t^2 is 'a comparison^2, divided by its variance'. But the 'comparison^2' is itself an estimate of variance, estimated from one comparison only, and therefore with one degree of freedom. So, if t has n degrees of freedom, $t_n^2 = F_{1,n}$, i.e. t^2 is a variance ratio with 1 and n degrees of freedom. That means that any t-test may equally well be done as an F-test. Once we have a table of F, a table of t is superfluous. For example (in Chapter 1) the test of male versus female gave a variance ratio of $4\cdot80/1\cdot20 = 4\cdot0$, and (in Chapter 2) the test of male versus female gave $t = 1\cdot60/0\cdot80 = 2\cdot0$, so, $t^2 = F$. The variance ratio test is more general than the t-test, because F can have more than one degree of freedom in the numerator, but the principle is the same: if there are no true biological effects to swell the numerator, F is the ratio of two independent estimates of the same variance, and so is expected to equal 1. As mentioned in Chapter 1, the word 'independent' is important, neither mean square may 'include' the other, or any part of the other. As a ridiculous extreme, if we used the same mean square as numerator and denominator, F would necessarily be exactly 1. Since the F-test is concerned with variances, it is not very robust, i.e. it is sensitive to non-Normality of the remainders (but if the numerator of F has only one degree of freedom, $F = t^2$, and so the F- and t-tests must be equally robust in that case). Sometimes, in a complicated analysis of variance, it is difficult to decide which mean square to use as denominator in an F-test. For example, in the two-way table of Chapter 2, we had the choice of comparing the 'rows' mean square with the 'interactions' mean square, or with the 'residual' mean square. However, the choice of an appropriate denominator is really quite simple. The test is intended to examine whether there are genuine differences between rows. It compares the actual value of the 'rows' mean square with an estimate of 'what the mean square would be, if there were no worthwhile differences between rows'. Then, if F is not significantly large, there is no reason to suppose that worthwhile differences between rows actually exist. So, when choosing a denominator for F, we need only ask, 'How big would we expect the numerator mean square to be, if no true biological effects (of the kind we are looking for) were present?' Then, as denominator, we use a 'residual' mean square which estimates the level of variation to be expected, in the absence of such biological effects. It is a part of good experimental design, to make sure that an appropriate 'residual' mean square shall indeed be available (Chap. 8).

The χ^2 test, also, may be treated as a special case of the variance-ratio test. The following argument shows how. Usually, the denominator of F is a 'residual' mean square which estimates the population variance V. Now suppose that the sample includes the whole (infinite) population. The denominator will have infinite degrees of freedom, and it will equal V exactly, because that is how V is defined. (This is a purely theoretical argument, because it is impossible to take an infinite sample, but sometimes (as in Example 1a, Chap. 9) we use a theoretical expected value as the denominator of F, and then we say that the denominator, being exact, has infinite degrees of freedom.) In that case, F becomes a numerator mean square (with n degrees of freedom, say) divided exactly by V. Unless it is inflated by true biological effects of the kind that are being tested, the numerator mean square will equal V on average. But, by definition of χ^2, the 'sum of squares $\div V$' has a χ^2 distribution with n degrees of freedom. Therefore, the 'mean square $\div V$' has the same distribution as χ_n^2/n. In other words, $F_{n,\infty}$ is the same as χ_n^2/n. Once again, therefore, the table of χ^2 becomes superfluous, once we have a table of F. Since χ^2 with n degrees of freedom is expected to equal n, χ_n^2 has to be quite a bit bigger than n, before it can be 'significant'.

The χ^2 distribution is very important in statistical theory, because it describes the behaviour of sums of squares of Normal deviates, and so underlies the whole theory of sums of squares, standard errors, etc. χ^2 has the important property of additivity. If y_i is Normal with mean m_i and variance V_i, $(y_i - m_i)^2/V_i$ is χ^2 with one degree of freedom. Its average value is 1, because V_i is defined as the average value of $(y_i - m_i)^2$. The sum of n such values, $\overset{n}{\Sigma}(y_i - m_i)^2/V_i$, is χ^2 with n degrees of freedom. Its average value is n. In other words, χ_n^2 is the sum of n independent values of χ_1^2; and the sum of χ^2 with n_1 degrees of freedom and an independent χ^2 with n_2 degrees of freedom, is χ^2 with $(n_1 + n_2)$ degrees of freedom. This is the familiar property that you can add together sums of squares, or, conversely, analyse a sum of squares into independent parts.

χ^2 is mostly used, in practice, to analyse counts, i.e. frequency distributions, contingency tables, etc. The usual expressions for χ^2 are really weighted sums of squares (Chap. 1). But counts are not distributed Normally, they must be positive whole numbers. Very often, it is good enough to treat the count *residuals* as approximately Normal. The calculated values of χ^2 then conform approximately to the theoretical distribution of χ^2, but we must look carefully for cases where the approximation breaks down. This is likely to happen when the average or expected count in any category is less than five. Such cases may be treated by the likelihood-ratio method discussed in Chapter 7.

Numerous pitfalls await us, when we use χ^2 to analyse contingency tables. To be sure that the χ^2 approximation can be trusted, we require that the expected (not the observed) value for each cell shall be at least five. The entries in a contingency table must be independent and complete. Suppose we take blood samples from 100 humans, of whom 47 are male. 31 are found to be Rhesus negative, of whom 17 are male. It would be wrong to construct the following table

	Humans	Males
Rh −	31	17
Rh +	69	30
Total	100	47

because the 'humans' column *includes* the 'males' column. It is essential to split the table instead, into independent entries.

	Females	Males	Total
Rh −	14	17	31
Rh +	39	30	69
Total	53	47	100

The table must also be *complete*. Suppose we wish to test the sex ratio for 1:1. It is wrong to say 'of 100 people, 50 males were expected, but 47 were observed, so $(47-50)^2/50$ is χ^2 with one degree of freedom'. It is essential to include the females as well:

Males	Females
47	53
(50 expected)	(50 expected)

Now, χ^2 (with 1 degree of freedom) is $(47-50)^2/50 + (53-50)^2/50$. Another difficulty concerns the combination of different contingency tables. For example, the two tables

80	20	and	10	10
----	----		----	----
20	5		40	40

reveal exact proportionality, the χ^2 (1 degree of freedom) for heterogeneity (i.e. disproportionality) being zero in both cases. However, if we injudiciously add the two tables together, we get a table which is very disproportionate:

$$
\begin{array}{cc|}
90 & 30 \\
60 & 45 \\
\hline
\end{array}
$$

This example shows that individual contingency tables may not be added together, except in particular circumstances. One way of combining the evidence from several separate tables, is to calculate a value of χ^2 for each table, and add together those values of χ^2 to get an overall χ^2. This method is sometimes unsatisfactory, because χ^2 takes no account of the *direction* of the heterogeneity. For example, the two tables

	Males	Females
Rh −	17	14
Rh +	30	39

and

	Males	Females
Rh −	14	17
Rh +	39	30

yield the same value of χ^2, but the first shows a slight (non-significant) excess of Rh negative males and Rh positive females, while the second table shows the reverse. Yates (1955) gives a better way of combining a set of 2 x 2 tables (see Example 2, this chapter).

Values of χ^2, calculated from frequency data, only approximate the true χ^2 distribution. Yates's correction for continuity improves the approximation. It may only be used when χ^2 has 1 degree of freedom, for example, in a 2 x 2 contingency table. Yates's correction should not be used when calculating values of χ^2 which will themselves be used in further calculations, e.g., added to other values of χ^2. It should be used only when the value of χ^2 will be used immediately to assess significance. In effect, Yates' correction calculates a wrong value of χ^2 which gives a correct estimate of the level of significance.

Although χ^2 gives a good *test* of heterogeneity, it is a poor *measure*. The two tables

$$
\begin{array}{cc|}
90 & 30 \\
60 & 45 \\
\hline
\end{array}
\quad \text{and} \quad
\begin{array}{cc|}
900 & 300 \\
600 & 450 \\
\hline
\end{array}
$$

show precisely the same degree of disproportion, yet χ^2 in the second table is ten times larger than in the first.

Significance Tests

Sometimes a value of t, F, or χ^2 is significantly *small* (say, $P > 95$ per cent). Such values are just as remarkable, in their way, as significantly large ones: they will, of course, occur by chance once in twenty times. But, if genuine, this result implies that *either* the test has been mis-applied, *or* the data have somehow been selected, or adjusted, to give a suspiciously exact answer, *or* some biological mechanism is acting to control variation.

Examples 6

(1) (a) From printed tables of t, F, and χ^2, verify that $t_n^2 = F_{1,n}$ and that $\chi_n^2/n = F_{n,\infty}$.

(b) Suppose that $\bar{y}_1$ and $\bar{y}_2$ are the means of two samples, each of N observations, with combined 'residual' mean square s^2. Show that, to test the difference between $\bar{y}_1$ and $\bar{y}_2$, $t = (\bar{y}_1 - \bar{y}_2)/\sqrt{(2s^2/N)}$ and $F = N(\bar{y}_1 - \bar{y}_2)^2/2s^2$, therefore, $t^2 = F$. This example confirms the statement in Chapter 1, that the 'between' mean square is indeed concerned with the average differences *between* categories.

(2) *Combination of 2 x 2 tables.* In samples of students in Australia and Canada, the numbers of horseowners were as follows.

| | Australia | | Canada | |
	Men	Women	Men	Women
Horse	14	23	4	11
No horse	14	9	29	19

Are men and women equally likely to own horses? Show that in the Australian table, $\chi_1^2 = 3 \cdot 023$ and in the Canadian, $\chi_1^2 = 5 \cdot 219$. These values are calculated without Yates's correction for continuity, because they will be used in further calculations.

(a) Adding together the two values of χ^2, we get $\chi_2^2 = 8 \cdot 242$. This takes no account of the *direction* of the deviation, i.e. of the fact that in *both* tables, there is an excess of women horseowners.

(b) Yates's (1955) method. χ^2 with one degree of freedom is, by definition, the square of a Normal deviate with zero mean and unit variance. Therefore, $\sqrt{3 \cdot 023} = +1 \cdot 739$ may be treated as Normal ($m = 0$, $V = 1$). Similarly, $\sqrt{5 \cdot 219} = +2 \cdot 285$ is Normal (0, 1). Both values are given the same sign to show that the deviation is in the same direction in both tables. If the deviations were in opposite directions, one sign (it does not matter which) would be taken positive, and the other negative. The sum $+1 \cdot 739 + 2 \cdot 285 = 4 \cdot 024$ is therefore Normal (0, 2), because the sum of two Normal variates is a Normal variate. $4 \cdot 024/\sqrt{2} = 2 \cdot 846$ is therefore Normal (0, 1). There are several ways of testing $2 \cdot 846$ as a Normal (0, 1) deviate. It can be compared with a table of the Normal distribution, or, equivalently, with a table of t with infinite degrees of freedom. Alternatively, $2 \cdot 846^2$ is χ^2 with one degree of freedom, which is equivalent to $F_{1,\infty}$.

Compare the results of (a) and (b). This method may be used to combine any number of 2 × 2 tables; but, just like χ^2 itself, Yates's method gives a good *test* of the existence of an effect, but a very bad *measure* of the size of the effect.

7 | SOME UNDERLYING THEORY

THIS is a difficult chapter; it digs into the logical principles which underlie everyday statistical methods. Rarely do we apply these principles *directly*, when deciding how to analyse any given case in practice, but some acquaintance, however slight, with principles can help to prevent serious mistakes. Unfortunately, under investigation, it very soon appears that statistical methods are built on 'mud'. This does not matter in practice, because the 'mud' is amply strong enough to bear the structure of everyday statistical methods. Statisticians agree well enough on what to do, but argue fiercely about why they do it. Statistical methods work in practice, but nobody has yet found a 'watertight' justification for making inferences. The same difficulty besets, not just statistics, but all scientific research. If we knew a foolproof logical justification for making inferences of any kind, we could apply it to statistical inference in particular, and vice versa. This chapter will consider only the statistical aspect of this wider problem.

Suppose we have a sample S which gives us some information about a parameter θ. Perhaps θ might be a population mean or a regression coefficient. Before the sample S is taken, we do not necessarily consider that all possible values of θ are equally probable. So we say that there is a prior probability $p(\theta_i)$ that θ shall equal any given value θ_i. Some people regard $p(\theta_i)$ as a personal assessment, peculiar to themselves, of all the possible values which θ can take: others regard $p(\theta_i)$ as reflecting the structure of the real world. Having obtained the sample S, we may use its information to update our assessment of θ, in other words, to convert the prior probabilities $p(\theta_i)$ into new probabilities which take account of the sample S. That is done by Bayes's Theorem, which says that the probability (in the light of S) that $\theta = \theta_i$, is proportional to $p(\theta_i)L(S|\theta_i)$. Here, $L(S|\theta_i)$ is the probability of obtaining the sample S, when $\theta = \theta_i$. ('$S|\theta_i$' does not mean 'S divided by θ_i', but 'S, given that $\theta = \theta_i$'.) $L(S|\theta_i)$ is known as the likelihood of obtaining S when

72

$\theta = \theta_i$; we shall use it to help us compare the different possible values of θ, in the light of the observed sample S.

Bayes's Theorem tells us to multiply the likelihood by the prior probability, in order to obtain a new assessment of the probability that $\theta = \theta_i$. It is here that the trouble starts. Nobody denies that Bayes's Theorem is algebraically correct. The disputes arise over its application. The likelihood $L(S|\theta_i)$ is perfectly well defined, and its value may be calculated for any S and θ_i. It is obtained from the probabilities of the individual observations which make up the sample S. But the theorem asserts that, before we can use $L(S|\theta_i)$ to compare the probabilities of different values of θ_i in the light of S, we must multiply $L(S|\theta_i)$ by the prior probability $p(\theta_i)$. We must therefore assign values to $p(\theta_i)$, for all values of θ_i. Some people (often called Bayesians) say that it is possible to do so; others disagree.

It could be that some previous experience (i.e. some previous sample) gives us information about θ; but Bayes's Theorem says that we cannot use that experience to give us values of $p(\theta_i)$ without the aid of some initial set of prior probabilities. However much experience we may have, the theorem requires us to return in time to a starting point, where we must assign prior probabilities $p(\theta_i)$ to different values of θ_i, when we are completely ignorant about θ. So a plea of 'previous experience' cannot extricate us from the dilemma — what is the value of $p(\theta_i)$, when we know nothing about θ? This dilemma is not very serious in practice. Suppose we are comparing two possible values of θ. As evidence accumulates, i.e. as the size of the sample S increases, the comparison comes to depend more and more on the likelihoods, which soon outweigh the prior probabilities. So it does not much matter, in practice, what values of $p(\theta_i)$ we adopt, provided that they are not ridiculously small or zero (that is, provided we admit that θ_i is a possible value of θ). However, to justify the whole process of statistical inference, we must — according to Bayes — find some way of assigning values to $p(\theta_i)$, when we know nothing about θ.

Some people argue that, when we know nothing about θ, all values of θ are equally possible, and so all values of $p(\theta_i)$ must be the same. There are many objections. For example, the argument seems to contradict itself. If $\phi = 1/\theta$, a uniform distribution of $p(\theta_i)$ implies a non-uniform distribution of $p(\phi_i)$; but we know nothing of ϕ, just as we know nothing of θ, so the distribution of $p(\phi_i)$ ought to be uniform too. But the greatest objection is that many people find the argument incredible. They flatly deny that, because we know nothing about θ, we can say that all possible values of θ are equally likely. If we consider $p(\theta_i)$ to be a personal, subjective assessment, different people may validly use different values for $p(\theta_i)$, in which case anyone may, at least in theory, validly draw any conclusion he chooses from a given set of evidence. If we consider $p(\theta_i)$ to be some kind of objective probability reflecting the real world, the values of $p(\theta_i)$ must be the same for everybody; but people disagree about the values to be used, in practice, when everybody is equally ignorant of θ. It may be argued that we are never completely ignorant about any possible question; even when we have no directly relevant evidence, our total experience can always give us some idea of what to expect. But vague experience cannot be turned into the precise numerical probabilities which Bayes's Theorem requires. To summarize, there is no indisputable way of assessing prior probabilities, but, in practice, any 'reasonable' set of prior probabilities will do.

Another school of thought, that of Fisher, admits the algebraic validity of Bayes's Theorem but denies its relevance to problems of statistical inference. The value of $p(\theta_i)$ is unknowable, and therefore cannot be used in practice. Some people go further, and deny that $p(\theta_i)$ exists at all. Instead, we remember that the likelihood $L(S|\theta_i)$ is, in fact, the likelihood of obtaining the observed sample S, given that $\theta = \theta_i$. Since the likelihood sums up all that we know about θ_i, we need consider only the likelihood itself. In particular, we take that value of θ_i which maximizes the likelihood to be the 'best' estimate of θ. It is obvious that maximizing $L(S|\theta_i)$ would be the same as maximizing $p(\theta_i)L(S|\theta_i)$, if $p(\theta_i)$ were the same for all values of θ_i. So the Bayesians say that Fisher's disciples delude themselves — the principle of maximum likelihood really uses Bayes's Theorem, with a hidden assumption that $p(\theta_i)$ is the same for all values of θ_i. Fisher's school replies that when we maximize the likelihood, we maximize the likelihood and nothing else. To accept the likelihood as supreme arbiter is a new basic principle. However gratifying its consequences may be, the principle itself has to be taken on trust.

There are still some technical problems, which arise whether or not we use prior probabilities. They concern the idea of 'sufficiency'. A sufficient estimate of θ, calculated from the values in the sample S, is one that absorbs all the information about θ contained in the sample. For example, if the values of y in the sample are Normally distributed, the sample can tell us nothing more about the population mean m, once we know the arithmetic mean $\bar{y}$ of the sample. The sample mean

$\bar{y}$ is a sufficient estimate of m. That is a very important idea, since it means that, once we have analysed a set of data in an appropriate way, it is useless to try alternative analyses in the hope of getting more information. In this case, once we know the arithmetic mean of the sample, we need not waste time trying to extract any further information about the population mean. Likelihood theory shows that, in those cases where it is possible to find a single sufficient estimate at all, the maximum likelihood estimate (i.e. the value of θ which maximizes the likelihood) will itself be sufficient. Whenever the distribution of y permits a sufficient estimate of θ, there is no problem; we use the maximum likelihood estimate, or some equivalent which may be more convenient to use in practice, confident that we cannot do better. But, for some distributions of y, no sufficient estimate of θ exists. In that case, although the likelihood still sums up all that the sample tells us about θ, no one estimate of θ can embody all that information. Fortunately, if y follows the basic distributions — Binomial and Poisson for counts, Normal for continuous measurements — the everyday estimates of means, regressions, etc. are sufficient.

As an example, we return to the equation $y_i = F_i +$ remainder, used in Chapter 1. Suppose that the remainder is Normally distributed with variance V_i. That means that the probability of obtaining a particular value y_i is proportional to $\exp[-(y_i - F_i)^2/2V_i]$. The likelihood of a sample of N different values of y is proportional to the product of the N individual probabilities, and so it is proportional to

$$\exp\left[-\sum_{}^{N}(y_i - F_i)^2/2V_i\right].$$ We remember that F_i might represent a mean, the same for all the ys, or perhaps a regression on some concomitant observation x_i. In either case, to estimate F_i by maximum likelihood, we need to maximize $\exp[-\Sigma(y_i - F_i)^2/2V_i]$, which is equivalent to minimizing the weighted sum of squares $\Sigma(y_i - F_i)^2/V_i$. Usually, V_i is the same for every y_i, in which case we minimize the unweighted sum of squares $\Sigma(y_i - F_i)^2$. So 'least squares' may be regarded, either as a principle in its own right (regardless of how y is distributed), or as a special case of maximum likelihood, which arises when the remainders are Normally distributed.

Now we can put together various points discussed in this book. Transformed scales of measurement are used to make the effects of treatments approximately additive, partly because we can think most easily in additive terms, and partly because statistical analyses are based on additive models. If the treatment effects are additive, it is quite

Some Underlying Theory

likely that the remainders will be nearly Normally distributed. Likelihood theory then justifies the use of least-squares estimates. Those estimates will be sufficient, and, in that sense, optimal. Least-squares estimates of means, regression coefficients, etc. are robust, so that the biological answer is not seriously affected by reasonable departures from Normality. All is well, provided that we can accept likelihood theory. That means that we must either arbitrarily accept the likelihood as supreme arbiter — a role which it usually performs very well — or use arbitrary prior probabilities in Bayes's Theorem.

Let us consider an example. A factory, mass-producing some product, needs to test each batch to check the quality of the articles. Very often, it is too expensive to test every item, so the factory takes a sample from each batch. If the sample is satisfactory, the batch is accepted; if not, it is rejected. A firm decision, to accept or reject, has to be made for every batch. Neyman and Pearson developed the theory of significance tests along analogous lines. A significance test, they say, must either accept or reject a null hypothesis (which might be, for example, that the population mean m is zero). The theory concerns the chances of making wrong decisions — of rejecting the null hypothesis when it is true, or of accepting it when it is false. Many statisticians accept the theory, but others agree with Fisher, who said that it is a false analogy. In scientific research, significance tests are not used to accept or reject hypotheses, but to assess the weight of evidence for, or against, them. We can never finally reject any hypothesis, however improbable it may become. Therefore, according to Fisher, analogy with decision making is not pertinent. Now let us consider what we actually do in practice. If the significance probability is large (greater than 1 per cent, say) we do not actually reject the null hypothesis, but assess it as unlikely; but, if the probability is small (1 in 1000 or less), we jump to certainty, and decisively reject the null hypothesis. Such behaviour cannot be logical, but is certainly rational. If you are being charged by an elephant, you should, logically, stop to assess the probabilities of all possible outcomes — for example, that the elephant might drop dead of heart failure — before deciding what to do, but, in practice, it would be advantageous to ignore improbable outcomes. Thus, Fisher's point of view is right when the significance is slight, but Neyman–Pearson theory is applicable when the significance is strong. We cannot say exactly where the transition from assessment to rejection occurs. It will, in any case, depend on the practical consequences of making a mistake, but the transition is made somewhere in between the customary arbitrary levels of 5 per cent, 1 per cent, and 0·1 per cent. That is why those standard levels were chosen in the first place.

A significance test assesses the probability of obtaining the result actually observed, supposing that the null hypothesis is true. It is customary to take into account, also, the probabilities of obtaining results more extreme than the one actually observed. If we say that the 5 per cent value of t is 1·96, we mean that the probability, on the null hypothesis, of obtaining that value of t *or one greater in size* is 5 per cent. However, Jeffreys (1939) pointed out the inconsistency of considering values which have not been observed — and which the null hypothesis declares to be improbable — when assessing the significance of the value that has actually been obtained. Another difficulty, trivial in practice but logically serious, is that definitions of 'more extreme' can sometimes be ambiguous or contradictory. (The F-test ought to become less stringent as the accuracy of its numerator and denominator increases. In general, it does. But if you look at a table of 5 per cent values of F with n and 2 degrees of freedom, you will see that the values of F actually *increase* as n increases. This anomaly itself shows that something is wrong.) Fisher (1959) accepted Jeffreys's objection. He proposed, in place of the usual type of significance test, to use the likelihood ratio as criterion. We have already noted that the likelihood $L(S|\theta)$ embodies the information conveyed by the sample S, about the unknown parameter θ. So if the likelihood decreases rapidly on either side of its maximum, we need only consider values of θ close to the maximum. Likelihood theory uses the rate of that decrease, to judge the accuracy of the estimate of θ. Suppose that somebody proposes, for our consideration, a null hypothesis that the true value of θ (in the population from which the sample S was drawn) is θ_0. To assess that hypothesis, we may use the ratio of $L(S|\theta)$, when $\theta = \theta_0$, to $L(S|\theta)$, when θ takes its maximum-likelihood value, i.e. to the maximum value of $L(S|\theta)$. That ratio cannot exceed 1, simply because θ is chosen to maximize $L(S|\theta)$. If the ratio is small, we shall suppose that the null hypothesis is unlikely, because alternative values of θ are much more likely. This significance test makes no reference to probabilities. Instead of arbitrary 5 per cent or 1 per cent probability levels, it substitutes arbitrary likelihood-ratio levels. Although this type of test avoids many of the difficulties which beset orthodox significance tests, it is not yet in general use. (Some existing tests convert the likelihood ratio into a corresponding probability, thereby exposing themselves to

Jeffreys's criticism.) Bayesians will not accept this likelihood-ratio test as it stands, because it ignores the prior probability of θ_0.

This chapter has examined, very briefly, some of the logical difficulties which beset statistical methods. The difficulties are not too serious, because the various approaches all lead to essentially the same practical recipes. Although orthodox significance tests may be a bit dubious logically, they work well enough in practice. However, the absence of a 'watertight' logical basis warns us that statistical methods are not foolproof, but must be used with commonsense.

Examples 7

(1) An insect parasite lays one egg in each of 100 larvae. Her progeny include 36 males and 64 females.
(a) Use χ^2 to test for $1:1$ sex ratio.
(b) Suppose the true (population) proportion of females is p. The observed fraction $64/100$ is an estimate of p. In a sample of N individuals, the variance of the estimate is $p(1-p)/N$. Use this variance to find the standard error of the estimate, for $N = 100$ and $p = 0.64$. Since this standard error is derived from theory, it has infinite degrees of freedom. Use $t = 1.96$ to find 95 per cent confidence limits for p.
(c) Find the angular transform (degrees) of the proportion of females. The variance of the angular transform is $820.7/N$, whatever the original value of p (Fisher and Yates 1953, Table XII). Find 95 per cent confidence limits on the transformed scale and convert them back to the original scale.
(d) Here is the likelihood treatment of the same problem. The probability of obtaining one female is p. The probability of obtaining 64 females is therefore the product of 64 ps, i.e. p^{64}. Similarly for the males. The likelihood L is therefore proportional to $p^{64}(1-p)^{36}$; and $\log L$ is $64 \log p + 36 \log(1-p)$. Calculate $\log L$ for $p = 0.52, 0.56, 0.60, 0.64, 0.68, 0.72$, and 0.76. (You can, if you wish, read the values of p as a variate into the computer, and make it calculate $\log L$ as a new variate.) By plotting $\log L$ against p, or by calculus, show that the maximum likelihood occurs when $p = 0.64$, which is therefore the maximum likelihood estimate of the proportion of females. It equals the proportion of females in the sample. Calculate the likelihood ratio, i.e. (L/the maximum L), for $p = 0.52, 0.56, 0.60 \ldots 0.76$, and plot it against p. Read off the values of p for which the likelihood ratio takes the arbitrary value $1/6$. Are those values of p (i) close to, (ii) the same as, the 95 per cent confidence limits in (b) or (c)? †

† If n_1 is the observed number of females, and n_2 the number of males, $\log L$ is $n_1 \log p + n_2 \log(1-p)$. That is exactly true, whatever n_1 and n_2 may be. The *expected* values of n_1 and n_2 are Np and $N(1-p)$. The *expected* value of $\log L$ is therefore proportional to $N[p \log p + (1-p)\log(1-p)]$. The expression in brackets is the 'information' (Chap. 9). Information theory is therefore an approximate, or large-sample, version of likelihood theory.

(2) Repeat Example 1 for a sample containing 97 females and 3 males. Try values of $p = 0.92$, 0.93, 0.96, 0.97, 0.98, and 0.99. In this case, p is so close to 1.0, that the confidence limits in (b) extend beyond $p = 1.0$.

8 | EXPERIMENTS AND SAMPLES

ONCE the design of an experiment has been decided, the method of analysis follows automatically (given a statistical model and remainder distribution). Before the advent of computers, experimental designs were chosen to make the analysis as easy as possible. Analysis of a badly designed experiment, using a desk calculator, can take many hours, but a computer can do any analysis, however complex. From that point of view, experimental design is no longer quite so important as it used to be. But there are three important provisos. Firstly, we naturally want to get as much information as possible, for a given amount of work. In other words, we want to maximize the accuracy of the experimental results. Secondly, we want to avoid non-orthogonality, with its attendant ambiguities (Chap. 2). And thirdly, we must avoid designs which cannot be analysed at all. For example, suppose we wish to try a new drug on some rats. Suppose, further, that we misguidedly give the drug only to female rats, and use only male rats as control. Then the drug-versus-control difference is completely confused, or 'confounded', with the female-versus-male difference, and no amount of statistical analysis can separate the two comparisons. An experiment must, therefore, be designed to give an unbiased estimate of differences between treatments. Chapter 6 said that, to test the significance of a treatment effect, we ought to use a 'remainder' mean square which will indicate how big the difference is expected to be, if the treatment has no real effect at all. An experimental design should, therefore, permit the estimation of an appropriate mean square. In technical language, the design must furnish a valid estimate of residual variance.

Both those purposes — unbiased estimates of treatment effects, and a valid estimate of residual variation — are served by randomization. Some people think that randomization is Fisher's answer to all statistical evils: it is not. Randomization only works on *average* — that is to say, a whole series of experiments, each with a different randomization, would, on average, give unbiased estimates of treatment effects and of residual variance. If we assign each rat to drug or control at random, there can *on average* be no intrinsic difference between the two sets of rats, because any rat is equally likely to appear in either set. But, in practice, we are only going to do one experiment involving one particular randomization. If we divide rats at random into two groups of size N, there is bound to be *some* difference between the two means. According to the usual rules (Chap. 2), the difference will, on average, be zero, with standard error $\sqrt{(2V/N)}$. Randomization is the best we can do, to avoid accidental bias, but, if the size N of each group is small, large intrinsic differences between groups may still occur by chance.

We use randomization to take care of *unpredictable* variation: but the experiment could be designed so that any treatment is applied to equal numbers of male and female rats. It would then be 'balanced' for sexes. We can only do that, because we can *recognize* males and females. Comparisons between treatments would then be free of sexual complications. Alternatively, animals might be assigned to treatments entirely at random, without regard to sex. Each treatment would receive approximately, but not exactly, equal numbers of males and females. Then, if there were important differences between the sexes, affecting the experimental results, the experiment would be less accurate, because the effects of sex would be mixed in with the effects of treatments. The sexes and treatments would not form an orthogonal two-way table (Chap. 2). Once a category (in this case, sex) has been recognized, its possible effects should be allowed for in the analysis (Example 5, Chap. 2).

Those, then, are the reasons why the biologist needs to consult the statistician *before* he does the experiment. Few biologists do so (which is perhaps fortunate for the overworked statistician). Very often, an experiment could have been done more efficiently. Occasionally, it cannot be analysed at all to obtain an answer to the questions which the biologist wanted to ask. When a biologist does consult a statistician about an experiment, it sometimes takes an hour to establish exactly what questions are to be asked, and five minutes to design an appropriate experiment. Here we meet the two overriding considerations in the design of experiments and samples. Firstly, if you think out, exactly and precisely, what questions you wish to ask, an appropriate design is, very often, obvious. Secondly, it is wise to consider how the results will be analysed, *before* the experiment is done. There is then less chance of omitting some vital measurement. Those two rules may seem trite, until you recognize their overwhelming cogency. It is very sad to find, too late, that the wrong question has been asked, or that something essential has not been measured. Admittedly, in truly exploratory research, it is often impossible to predict exactly what measurements will prove to be essential. There is, therefore, a temptation to measure everything in sight, in the hope that it may come in useful. It may certainly be a good idea to include any extra measurements which can be obtained cheaply. That must be a matter for personal decision, but 'the idea of compiling massive routine records in the hope that they will eventually be of value in retrospective research is nearly always disappointing in practice, though useful suggestions and indications may be obtained' (Bailey 1967). It is common experience that large masses of data, previously collected for some other purpose, rarely afford much information about some new question.

The discussion, so far, applies equally to experiments and samples. What, then, is the difference between the two? The difference is causality. When we do an experiment, we ourselves specify which units (e.g. rats) shall receive which treatments, and we try to ensure, by randomization, that the effects of those treatments cannot be confused, or confounded, with any other extraneous effects. We are, therefore, entitled to assert, that the treatments which we applied *caused* the observed effects. In a sample survey, on the other hand, we can only observe relations. For example, the density of vole populations is correlated with the sodium content of the soil. While we may reasonably use the sodium content to *predict* the numbers of voles, we cannot validly say that the sodium *determines* the vole numbers — both might be caused by some third agent. Only when we ourselves can decide how the treatments are applied (or, as occasionally in genetics, when a natural randomization is done for us), may we assert causality. There are two provisos here. Firstly, as in the case of smoking and lung cancer, purely circumstantial evidence may become so overwhelming in favour of some reasonable hypothesis that we should be foolish to deny causality. That argument is admittedly illogical, but it is rational (Chap. 7). Secondly, causality is a human notion, unknown to the universe at large. I do not wish to become involved in philosophy, but, in a complex multivariate case, we may need to consider exactly what we mean by 'causality'. This point is especially relevant to ecologists who try to unravel complex natural relationships.

In a sample, just as in an experiment, the units are chosen with some degree of randomness. The reason is the same as before — to permit a valid estimate of remainder variance. Chapter 3 said that the values of x in a regression may be anything we choose. Therefore, in a sample (or experiment) taken to estimate a regression, the randomization need concern only the ys. The x values may be deliberately chosen, either for practical convenience or to improve the accuracy of the estimated regression. This raises the question, How big should the sample be? Consider the simple case of a comparison of two treatments. If each mean is based on N observations, and the difference between the two means is d, the standard error of d is $\sqrt{(2V/N)}$, and therefore (assuming Normality) $d/\sqrt{(2V/N)} = t$. Therefore, if we can guess approximately what the residual variance V will be, we can work out what value of N is required to render 'significant' any value of d which we care to specify. In other words, we can work out the sample size needed, on average, to detect a treatment difference of any specified size. A more sophisticated version of this method will work out the (larger) sample size needed to make it 95 per cent certain that a specified treatment difference will be detectable (e.g. Cochran and Cox 1957). If N turns out to be small, it may be necessary to increase it in order to get a reasonable number of degrees of freedom. If we look at a table of t, we see that the values are very large when the degrees of freedom are few, but that the values of t do not change very much once there are twelve or more degrees of freedom. So we try to ensure that the 'residual' mean square shall have at least twelve degrees of freedom. Occasionally, when dealing with very expensive or scarce material (e.g. large animals), we have to make do with very few degrees of freedom, and the experiment (or sample) suffers accordingly. But the trouble is that we must have some initial idea of the size of the residual variance V. Very often, we can guess from previous experience, but if we have no idea how much variance there will be, it is quite impossible to decide in advance how big N should be, to give a specified accuracy. It may be necessary to do some preliminary work to assess the amount of variation. Sequential methods offer a way round the difficulty. In a sequential experiment, or sample, the work is done in a series of unit steps, and is discontinued as soon as enough evidence has accumulated about the question that is being asked. This idea is very attractive, because it minimizes the amount of work required. There are several reasons why it is not often used in biological research. Firstly, although the variance V need not be known in advance, the type of remainder distribution must be known. A sequential scheme, intended for use on a population with a Poisson distribution, will go wrong if the distribution is, in fact, negative Binomial. Secondly, sequential schemes are designed to distinguish between pre-selected hypotheses, i.e. to accept one and reject the others. But chapter 7 pointed out that research workers sometimes want to assess a situation, rather than jump to conclusions. Thirdly, it is found in practice that, while sequential methods can economically distinguish between *categories*, sequential methods of *estimation* save very little work. If we want to estimate 'how many insects are on this tree' with some specified degree of accuracy, the necessary sequential and fixed-size samples will be approximately the same size; but if we only want to categorize 'there are a lot *or* very few insects', it may pay to use a sequential sample. It is easy to see why. If there are, in fact, a lot of insects present, only a small effort will be needed to establish the fact. In that case, the sequential sample will stop short, whereas a fixed-size sample (which has to be large enough to detect 'very few insects') will waste a lot of work. However, the overriding objection to sequential methods is the time they take. Consider an experiment on the growth of annual plants. A sequential scheme requires us to grow a few plants this year; a few next year; and so on until enough have been grown altogether. It is much quicker to grow a large number all at once, even if it turns out that it was not necessary to grow all of them. In biological research, most situations are like that, but in rare cases (e.g. genetics of microorganisms, which have a very short life-cycle, or surveys of insect abundance) sequential methods can sometimes save a lot of work.

It is worth taking some trouble over the way data are recorded. If we simply write the observations down on odd pieces of paper, we will find that some items are lost, or are not identifiable. It is very important to label data well, so that there can be no doubt later on as to what the numbers represent. Data should be written down in a format which will make them easy to use subsequently. If the observations are going to be extensive, specially designed forms can be very useful; they make the data easily accessible, and immediately reveal omissions. Such forms should leave space for working notes, for corrections, and for extra measurements which you may subsequently decide to make. Writing should be in ink, not pencil; mistakes should be crossed out, not overwritten. Sometimes the data can be recorded ready for computer input (written on computer data sheets, or punched directly on cards or tape). Sooner or later, computers will be able to read hand-written characters as a standard method of input. Until then, there is one cardinal principle. If a mechanical method of recording is used, it must give an instantaneous *printed* record, so that mistakes can be recognized and corrected in good time. Unfortunately, there exists no satisfactory portable hand-operated card, or tape, punch for use in the field. Fully automatic recording devices can be useful, but they are not necessarily the ideal in research work. They are expensive, they have to be constantly checked, they destroy the scientist's intimate acquaintance with his data, and they may be superfluous. For example, daily maximum and minimum temperatures are often just as good as continuous temperature records. Once again, the overriding consideration is, 'How am I going to use the data?'

Examples 8

(1) In Example 2 (Chap. 2) the 'residual' mean square (omitting the erroneous value) was 0·00410. How many pigs per treatment are needed to detect an average difference of (a) 0·05 and (b) 0·01 cm per day between two treatments, using the 5 per cent value of t?

DISTRIBUTIONS, INDICES OF DIVERSITY, AND INFORMATION

IN the last thirty years, many papers have been published on the fitting of special distributions. For example, we could have examined the distribution, in a sample of insects, of the numbers of individuals per species, or, perhaps, the numbers of species per quadrat, in a sample of plants. The analysis was intended to serve two purposes. Firstly it was hoped that, by showing that a given sample conformed to a negative Binomial, a LogNormal, a Hypergeometric, or an Exponential distribution, we could deduce something about the underlying biology which gave rise to that distribution. Secondly, biologists wanted to measure an 'index of dispersion' which would represent the properties of the distribution, so permitting comparison of one sample with another.

The first of these purposes was over-optimistic. Suppose that some distribution turns out to be negative Binomial. We know now that a negative Binomial distribution can arise in many different ways; Southwood (1966) mentions five. So we cannot deduce how the observed distribution arose in practice. To determine this, we must investigate the biological process. The study of distributions does not give quick biological information.

There is also a technical problem — it is very hard to establish that a given sample belongs to some particular distribution and to no other. If the counts were homogeneous, differing from each other only by chance, we should expect them to show a Poisson distribution. The Poisson distribution has only *one* parameter, the mean m. It is easy to estimate m — we use, in fact, the average sample count (except when a zero category, e.g. the number of species not represented in a sample at all, cannot be counted; in that case, estimation of m is more complicated). We can then compare the observed distribution of counts with the expected Poisson distribution. The variance of a Poisson distribution is equal to the mean m. Thus, the comparison may be made quickly, by comparing the variance of the sample counts with the estimate of m (Example 1, this chapter), or it can be made more thoroughly, by a χ^2 test of goodness-of-fit of frequencies. If the distribution is not of the Poisson type, it may be under-dispersed, i.e. have a variance less than its mean, implying that some control process is acting to reduce the variability; an example is the number of chiasmata per chromosome in a set of homologous chromosomes. Alternatively, the distribution may be over-dispersed, with variance greater than the mean, in which case the counts cannot be homogeneous; different counts are different, not purely by chance, but because of heterogeneity, either in the underlying biology, or in the method of sampling. Whereas the Poisson distribution has only one parameter, any under- or over-dispersed distribution will require at least two parameters, to give the right values for the mean and variance. A theoretical distribution with *two* adjustable parameters can be made to fit a much wider range of observed distributions than can the Poisson. In practice, it is often easy to show that a given sample does not obey a Poisson distribution, but difficult to prove that it is not (say) distributed negative Binomially. It may take a sample of several hundred counts to distinguish between a negative Binomial and a logarithmic type of distribution. And when we have such a large number of counts, they often do not conform to any of the standard distributions. Therefore, it is difficult, in practice, to identify a particular distribution with any certainty. Nor is there much point in so doing. It is useful to show that the observed distribution is not of the Poisson type, since that implies some kind of non-randomness. What causes the non-randomness is then a biological, not a statistical, problem. It is useless to fit (say) a negative Binomial distribution, unless the parameters of that distribution are to be subjected to further analysis. The negative Binomial distribution is then used simply as shorthand to sum up the observed set of counts. It would not much matter if the true distribution were not of the negative Binomial type at all, provided that it cannot be distinguished from one in practice. There is an amusing special case (Williams 1964). If a series of taxonomists (some 'splitters' and some 'lumpers') worked in succession on a family whose members actually showed purely random variation, the resultant distribution of numbers of species per genus would be logarithmic. That is precisely the distribution actually found in taxonomy. In justice to taxonomists, we must remember that a given distribution can arise in more than one way.

Although we no longer expect to use distribution statistics to get biological information easily, we still want to compare one distribution with another. If the distributions are of the Poisson type, we can

Distributions, Indices of Diversity, and Information

compare their means. But if the distributions are over-dispersed — in biology, they usually are — we need an index of diversity to measure the degree of dispersion. If we consider the distribution of a single species, we talk about an index of dispersion; if we consider the composition of a whole flora, we talk about an index of diversity. An obvious candidate is the sample variance, or perhaps the coefficient of variation (Example 1, Chap. 4). However, suppose we are dealing with a set of sample quadrats of a plant population. We want an index which shall characterize not just the sample, but the whole population. In other words, the index must be unaffected by the number or size or shape of the quadrats. That is very difficult. Before we can be sure that a given index is unaffected by the sampling procedure, we need to know the distribution, not just of the sample values, but of the original population — but usually, all we know of the population comes from the sample itself. Supposing we have calculated an index of diversity, what can we do with it? It can only be used to compare two different populations, and that can only be done safely when the two populations are sampled in the same way. So the idea of an *absolute* index of dispersion may not be very useful in practice. Greig–Smith (1964) discusses indices of dispersion and diversity at length.

One possible index is the measure of 'information'. Suppose that the individual units of a sample are sorted into categories. For example, individual animals might be sorted into their different species. If the frequency of the ith category is p_i, the 'information' is $-\Sigma p_i \log_2 p_i$. This is the measure of information used in communications engineering (it is different from, although related to, Fisher's definition of information in statistical theory). This measure of information is very closely related to entropy in statistical mechanics, and to likelihood in statistical theory. But there is an important practical difference. In communications theory, the information measures how much information we ourselves have to supply, on average, to specify a given message (and similarly, in statistical mechanics, the entropy measures our own ignorance of the energies of individual molecules); but, in statistics, the likelihood sums up the information which the sample gives to us.

The information $-\Sigma p_i \log_2 p_i$ is the average number of choices (or guesses) needed to allocate an individual to its category. Suppose we have three categories A, B, and C with frequencies $\frac{1}{2}$, $\frac{1}{4}$, and $\frac{1}{4}$. Then $-(\frac{1}{2} \log_2 \frac{1}{2} + \frac{1}{4} \log_2 \frac{1}{4} + \frac{1}{4} \log_2 \frac{1}{4})$ is $\frac{3}{2}$. We wish, by a series of guesses, to allocate a new individual to its proper category. We first ask, 'Is it

A?' If the answer is yes, we have found the right category with one guess. The probability of that happening is $\frac{1}{2}$. If the answer is no, we must ask a further question, 'Is it B?' The answer will decide between B and C, since we know beforehand that there are only three categories. Thus it takes two questions to identify B or C, and the extra question will be needed, on average, in $\frac{1}{2}$ of all cases. So the average number of questions necessary is $\frac{1}{2} \times 1 + \frac{1}{2} \times 2 = \frac{3}{2}$, which is the 'information' required, on average, to distinguish A, B, and C. It tells us how much information we ourselves must supply to specify an individual's category. It does not tell us how much information a sample contains about some question which we should like to ask. It is a long-term average, since in no case can we have exactly $\frac{3}{2}$ guesses.

It is quite another matter when we use the same function $-\Sigma p_i \log p_i$ as an index of diversity. Taking a sample of N individuals, we allocate each to a category, with n_i in the ith category. Then, $p_i = n_i/N$. The more categories there are, and the more evenly the individuals are scattered among the categories, the greater is the value of $-\Sigma p_i \log p_i$. So that value is indeed a measure of the diversity of the sample. But the value is no longer a long-term average, and no longer has a theoretical interpretation as an absolute measure of our uncertainty about the identity of an individual. The values of p_i are estimates from a small sample. If we increased the sample size N, we should expect to encounter new categories, not represented in the existing sample. The estimated value $-\Sigma p_i \log p_i$ may, or may not, be a good measure of the diversity of the population. There is no longer any theoretical backing to show that it is the absolute measure. By analogy, it is an attractive candidate as an index of diversity, but it must be treated, in practice, with the same caution as any other index.

Whereas animal ecology is all about population dynamics, energy flows, etc. plant ecology has been largely concerned with patterns of vegetation. That is why plant ecologists love indices of dispersion and diversity. It seems likely, however, that plant ecology will pay more attention to dynamic aspects in future.

Examples 9

(1) The number of bacterial colonies was counted on each square centimeter of an agar medium.

Number of colonies (y)	0	1	2	3	4	5	6	7	8
Observed frequency	59	86	49	30	16	2	0	1	1

Distributions, Indices of Diversity, and Information

The sample contains 59 values $y = 0$, 86 values $y = 1$, and so on.

(a) Show that the sample mean of y is 1·488, and the mean square 1·773. If the distribution is Poisson, the variance equals the mean. Test the variance ratio 1·773/1·488 — how many degrees of freedom?

(b) The probability of counting r colonies, when the mean is m, is $e^{-m} m^r/r!$ if the distribution is Poisson. The estimated value of m is 1·488. Show that the *expected* frequencies are

0	1	2	3	4	5 or more
55·12	82·00	60·99	30·25	11·25	4·39

Compare the observed and expected frequencies by χ^2. The value of χ^2 will have four degrees of freedom — why?

Methods (a) and (b) both test for a Poisson distribution. Using a desk calculator, (b) takes longer than (a), but it is more thorough, because it checks the whole distribution, not just the variance. However, it is unlikely — although not impossible — that a distribution of counts should differ seriously from the Poisson, if its variance equals its mean. Moreover, the value of χ^2 in (b) usually (as in this case) has rather few degrees of freedom, whereas there are plenty of degrees of freedom in (a). It is true that the variance-ratio test is inexact (why?), but so is the χ^2 test. To summarize, the variance ratio is usually quite good enough to test for a Poisson distribution, and it is quicker than the ponderous χ^2 test.

10 | QUANTITATIVE GENETICS

T H E R E are four fields of biology which rely heavily on their own peculiar brands of mathematics. (I am not counting subjects like thermodynamics or transport processes, which apply the mathematics of physics to biological situations.) They are enzyme kinetics, population genetics, population ecology, and quantitative genetics. The last three overlap in their content.

The theory of enzyme kinetics has reached a transitional stage. The general mathematical principles of enzyme reactions were established by 1930. Since then, the theory has been elaborated until the mathematics became intractable. The study of the *control* of enzyme systems, however, is still in its infancy. Not enough is yet known about the action of inhibitors, repressors, and hormones to permit reliable mathematical treatment of whole systems of enzymes. But that will come soon.

Population genetics has generated a considerable body of simple mathematics, mainly supplied by Fisher, Haldane, and Wright. More complicated work with computers has produced very few results which could not be expected from the earlier theory. Field work has revealed many natural genetic polymorphisms, e.g. in snails, butterflies, humans, *Drosophila*, rabbits, sheep, and cats, but the ecological pressures which maintain those polymorphisms are very incompletely understood, if at all. Population geneticists are therefore looking to ecology for the next step.

In their turn, some ecologists suspect that genetic differences between individuals may seriously affect the ecology of a population. If the population shows a Mendelian polymorphism, the theory of population genetics is applicable, or, at any rate, it ought to be. More often, there are no Mendelian genes in sight, or their relevance to ecological questions is unknown. The relevant ecologic variables, e.g. birth and survival, show a continuous range of variation. The appropriate branch of genetics is therefore 'quantitative inheritance'.

Quantitative Genetics

Population ecology presents many formidable mathematical problems, but those problems are trivial in comparison with our ignorance of population biology. At present, we just do not know how to do ecological research in order to provide the practical answers which are, more and more, expected of ecologists. It is as if we were trying to build dynamos with a science still at the iron-filings stage. Chapter 11 considers some aspects of the mathematics of populations, but does not present a coherent story, because no realistic theory yet exists. We do not even know if such a theory is possible.

The position of quantitative genetics is quite different. The subject has been intensively studied for fifty years. It has reached a stage where some things are possible, but others are demonstrably not. This chapter is a candid assessment of our understanding of quantitative inheritance.

Quantitative genetics studies the inheritance of characters which show a continuous range of variation. Each y value is influenced by the combined effect of numerous different genes, whose individual contributions are not distinguishable. In other words, it is not possible to determine the genotype by looking at the phenotype. The basic question is, 'If I am so tall and my spouse is so tall, how tall will our children be?' The answer must depend partly on genetic, and partly on environmental effects. Therefore, the simplest possible model is

phenotypic value of y = a genetic effect + an environmental effect. (10.1)

Now suppose that we have a one-way table, in which the different 'treatments' are different genotypes. In other words, there is a set of different genotypes, each represented by several individuals. From eqn (10.1) it follows that

> 'treatments' mean square is expected to equal a genetic component of variance + an environmental component of variance,
>
> 'residual' mean square is expected to equal the environmental component only. (10.2)

This is a simple example of 'components of variance', mentioned in Chapters 2 and 4. By subtracting the 'residual' mean square from the 'treatments' mean square, we get an estimate of the genetic component of variance. If, as occasionally happens, the 'treatments' mean square is actually less than the 'residual', the genetic component of variance comes out negative, which is unfortunate. The genetic component, expressed as a fraction of the 'genetic + environmental' components, is called the heritability, because it indicates how much of the variance of individuals is heritable. For technical reasons, the analysis is slightly more complicated than the above, but the principle is the same.

The estimate of heritability relies heavily on the truth of eqn (10.1). But eqn (10.1) asserts that, if two genotypes are grown side-by-side in a series of different environments, the difference in performance of those two genotypes will always be the same. That is demonstrably false. Genotype A may do better than genotype B in one environment, and worse in another. Genotypes and environments 'interact', (Chap. 2), and so eqns (10.1) and (10.2) ought to include interactions.

Having estimated a heritability, we still cannot use it to predict anything, because eqn (10.1) does not say how the genetic effect will be transmitted from generation to generation. To use the heritability in practice, we have to interpret it in terms of the effects of individual genes. This is where the trouble starts. The effects of individual genes are so well mixed that it is not possible to identify particular genes in particular individuals. The model of eqn (10.1) is extended by assuming that the genetic effect is the *additive* sum of the effects of the individual genes which affect y. There is no biological reason why that should be true. On the contrary, the growth of an individual is a highly coordinated process, so that there is every reason to expect that interactions between gene effects will be as important as the effects themselves. The additive model is used solely because it leads to tractable algebra. The theory was worked out by Fisher (1918). Fisher's almost incomprehensible paper contains all the essential theory; subsequent work has merely applied that theory in different ways.

We can now see why quantitative genetics relies heavily on the analysis of variances *per se*, in spite of the statistical objection that estimates of variance are not accurate or robust (Chap. 4). To make predictions from one generation to the next, we need to know something about the effects of individual genes. Compare the case of a lot of genes, each with small effect, and the case of a few genes of large effect. The *mean* $\bar{y}$ will be the same in both cases, but the *variance* will differ. So we are forced to analyse variances *per se*, if we want information about individual gene effects.

Assuming that gene effects are additive, and assuming further that mating is random — i.e. that different genes are assorted randomly — the heritability may be used to predict how much a population will respond to selection pressures (Falconer 1961). These predictions are the only real test of the theory, for the following reason. If it proves impossible to interpret the observed variances in terms of the strictly additive model, it is a simple matter to put in some interactions between genes, or between genes and environment. There is no limit to the number of interactions that can be invoked. That part of the variance, which can be interpreted as arising from additive effects of genes, is then called the 'additive genetic variance'. It is commonly, but quite fallaciously, supposed that the argument is reversible, i.e. that the 'additive genetic variances' estimated in real life must arise from additive effects of genes. But, if genetic interactions are as large as the additive effects, there is no point in thinking in terms of additive effects (Chap. 2). So the theory must make satisfactory predictions, partly as a test that we are on the right lines, and partly because that theory is otherwise useless in practice. Unfortunately, it is very often found that responses to selection are less than predicted (e.g. Falconer 1961, Moll and Robinson 1966, Penny *et al.* 1963, and Sheldon 1963). Indeed, there is even a special term, 'realized heritability', which means 'what the heritability ought to have been, to predict the right answer'.

Some selection experiments show diminishing returns, i.e. the response to selection gets less and less, the longer that selection is applied. It is, therefore, reasonable to try a non-additive model which includes an effect of 'diminishing returns'. When the strength of the 'diminishing returns' effect is nil, the new model is identical with the orthodox additive model. The new model may, therefore, be used to see how sensitive the orthodox model is to failure of the assumption that genes act additively (Gilbert 1961*a*). There is no need to go into details, here; briefly, the orthodox model does rely quite heavily on its assumption of additive gene action, but the new model cannot reasonably interpret some of the gross failures of selection that have been observed. We know that, in fact, very large interactions between gene effects do occur (Gilbert 1961*b*, Spickett and Thoday 1966); and Allard *et al.* (1972) have observed a very strong non-random association between genes in a natural population, which the additive analysis cannot detect. This all means that attempts to deduce information about the effects of individual genes are quite unreliable, partly because of the statistical unreliability of variances, and partly because the genetic model is unrealistic. By vigorous manipulation, it is possible to fit an additive model to almost any situation. But it is quite another thing to say 'the data can be explained in this way *and in no other*'. Expressions like 'additive genetic variance' are very misleading if taken literally. Quantitative genetics is a prime example of the danger (discussed in Chapter 4) that over-confidence in an additive model will lead the biologist to believe that he understands the true genetical situation. We need to admit that gene effects are too complex for realistic statistical analysis, unless the individual genes can be recognized.

There are two methods of analysis which make no assumptions about gene effects, and which do not rely on the dissection of variances. The first is offspring—parent regression. This is the ordinary regression of (say) the heights of sons on the heights of their fathers. Galton first used the curious term 'regression' because the sons of outstandingly tall fathers tend to revert, or 'regress', towards the mean height of the population. Assuming that it is not seriously diluted by errors of measurement (Chap. 3), the regression coefficient is a purely statistical measure of the genetical influence of fathers on sons. It is complicated by the fact that tall men tend to marry tall women. The other method of analysis is by 'combining abilities'. If y_{ij} is measured on the progeny of the ith male and the jth female, the model is

$$y_{ij} = m + a_i + b_j + \text{interaction} + \text{remainder},$$

where a_i, b_j are the 'combining abilities' of the two parents. This is the same model — and therefore the same analysis — as is used in a two-way table (Chap. 2). The method is most often used on plants, with a genetical assumption that $a_i = b_i$, i.e. that no distinction need be made between male and female parents. If the same individuals act as both male and female parents, the analysis is not quite the same as that of an ordinary two-way table (Yates 1947, Gilbert 1967). These two methods of analysis are both reliable, provided that no detailed genetical interpretation is forced onto them.

What is the point of studying quantitative genetics? There is a genetical interest in showing that the inheritance of quantitative characters can be explained by the hypothesis of multiple genes, so that there is no reason to suppose that the genetics are not essentially Mendelian. Fisher (1918) demonstrated that fact. There is also an intrinsic interest in trying to unravel the effects of the individual genes, but we now realize that that is a vain hope, except where special genetical methods are used. (Some people still do not accept that conclusion.) The practical applications lie in the fields of plant and animal breeding and of population ecology. Until recently, breeders hoped that quantitative genetics could furnish information about gene effects, which would reveal the best plan of breeding work. That hope has proved vain, but the purely statistical methods (offspring—parent regression and combining abilities) are sometimes useful, if only to analyse the results of crosses which have already been made for some other reason. It does not usually pay a breeder to examine a genetical situation in detail, if he has to wait a long time for the answers. But some kind of analysis is essential for characters which cannot be examined directly, e.g. the merit of a bull for milk production. In ecology, more and more attention is being paid to genetic variability within populations. The difficulty is to find anything to measure. Either the ecologist must opt for some Mendelian attribute (e.g. globulin electrophoretic patterns) of doubtful relevance to his main interests, or he must apply the methods of quantitative genetics to such things as number of offspring. Very often, the ecologist is not interested in genetical mechanisms at all, but merely wants to predict the performance of offspring from that of their parents. In that case, the statistical methods mentioned above are all that he needs.

Example 10

(1) Eqn (10.2) divides the 'treatments' mean square into a genetic component of variance + an environmental component of variance. The estimate of the genetic component may, with bad luck, come out negative. On the other hand, in an analysis of variance, the total sum of squares is divided into a 'treatments' sum of squares and a 'residual' sum of squares, neither of which can possibly be negative. Explain the difference.

11 | ANIMAL POPULATIONS

THIS chapter discusses some troublesome points in the mathematics of animal populations. It does not pretend to cover the whole field. In this chapter, the word 'population' means a lot of real live animals, not just a statistical abstraction.

There are several methods of estimating the size of a natural population. Southwood (1966) discusses them. It is rarely possible to make a complete count of all the animals in a given area. All the indirect methods of estimating population size depend on various working assumptions. For example, the capture—recapture method assumes that all animals in the population (or at any rate, in some recognizable category) have the same probability of capture. It seems unlikely that that can actually be true in any real case, although it may be near enough true to guarantee the method. Some methods of estimation have been tested on populations of known size, and sometimes the assumptions broke down so badly that the estimates were quite hopelessly wrong. Some, but not all, assumptions can be tested on internal evidence, in any given case. At present, it seems that no population estimates can be taken very seriously, unless two or three independent methods of estimation give similar answers. The doubtfulness of the assumptions means that, whatever you may think of the population estimates themselves, calculated standard errors of those estimates are little more than a bad joke; except that they provide a lower limit to the true error that can be expected. Fortunately, in many cases, there is not much point in estimating population numbers at all. We are much more interested in birth- and survival-rates, which are often more reliable than total numbers. For example, in a chain of capture-recapture samples, the estimate of population size depends critically on the assumption, mentioned above, of equal probabilities of capture, but the survival-rate is estimated by following the fortunes of a group of marked animals. There is then a secondary assumption, not used in the estimation process itself, that the survival of marked animals truly represents the survival of all animals in the population.

Animal Populations

The next few paragraphs will consider various ways of analysing fluctuations in population size. Suppose that the population size at time T is estimated to be N_T. Very often, the logarithmic transformation $\log N_T$ is used; very often this is an appropriate transform, because natural factors (climate, predation, etc.) tend to act multiplicatively on N_T. The logarithm converts birth- and survival-rates which, by definition, act multiplicatively, into additive factors (Chap. 5). That is why we use survival-rates, rather than death-rates. But, although birth- and survival-rates are very useful concepts, they are human abstractions which mean nothing to individual animals. There is no natural law which says that the logarithm is the perfect transform. By overlooking that fact, some authors have led themselves to erroneous conclusions.

Suppose we have a series of estimates of N_T at successive times T. The over-all population survival, from time T to $T + 1$, is N_{T+1}/N_T. Its logarithm is $(\log N_{T+1} - \log N_T)$. Key-factor analysis applies ordinary regression analysis to the fluctuations in $\log N_T$, or in $(\log N_{T+1} - \log N_T)$. Key-factor analysis comes in two forms. The first (Morris 1953) is a multiple regression of $\log N_{T+1}$ (as y-variate) on $\log N_T$ and on various natural factors (e.g. weather, food supply, predators) which might be relevant. The object is to see which of those factors may determine the size of N_{T+1}, so that the important factors may be investigated in detail. The second (Varley and Gradwell 1960) expresses the annual logarithmic survival $(\log N_{T+1} - \log N_T)$ as the sum of the logarithmic survivals during intermediate periods. The object is to see which of those intermediate periods plays the greatest part in determining the over-all survival, so that those intermediate survivals may be investigated in detail. Both types of analysis use the same values of N_T successively as y- and x-variates, but that technical objection is not very serious in practice, provided that about fifteen or more successive values of N_T are used. Both types try to use regression analysis to investigate determination (Chap. 3). Both methods consider only the fluctuations in population size; the natural factors which determine variations in N_T need not be those which decide its average level. Both methods can direct the biologist's attention to 'key factors', but only when a chain of estimates of N_T has been accumulated. A much more dubious type of analysis is the auto-regression of $\log N_T$ on itself, to estimate the degree of density dependence. The principle of density dependence says that life gets more difficult for individual animals as the population increases, and vice versa. There has been a long and futile argument about its validity, but most people now take the principle for granted — Haldane called it 'a blinding glimpse of the obvious'. A density-dependent effect need not act all the time on a given population. The auto-regression analysis depends on the following theory. Starting at any value of $\log N_T$ (whatever it may be), a completely density-dependent population will, on average, change the value of $\log N_{T+1}$ back to the long-term norm. Therefore, the value of $\log N_{T+1}$ will be unrelated to the value of $\log N_T$. So the regression coefficient b of $\log N_{T+1}$ on $\log N_T$ should be zero. But if there is no density dependence, $\log N_{T+1}$ will remain the same as $\log N_T$ except for 'accidental' fluctuations; therefore, the value of b should (so the theory goes) be 1. The actual value of b is supposed to indicate the actual degree of density dependence. It will evidently depend on the time interval between T and $T+1$. If that interval is very short compared with the time necessary for density-dependent factors to operate, $\log N_{T+1}$ will necessarily be close to $\log N_T$, and, therefore, b will be close to 1; but, if the interval is long, we shall expect little correlation between $\log N_T$ and $\log N_{T+1}$, even in a density independent situation.

Instead of b, some authors use the regression of the logarithmic survival $\log (N_{T+1}/N_T)$ on $\log N_T$. Since $\log (N_{T+1}/N_T)$ equals $(\log N_{T+1} - \log N_T)$, its regression equals $b - 1$. The two regressions are equivalent. There are several technical objections. Firstly, the same values of $\log N_T$ appear successively as y- and x-variates. As before, that will not seriously prejudice the value of b, provided that about fifteen or more successive values of N_T are used. But the use of $\log N_T$ as both x and y makes the usual standard error of b completely invalid, however long the chain of values may be (Moran 1952). Secondly, the regression coefficient b underestimates the true 'functional relation' (Chap. 3). That may or may not be serious, depending on the errors of estimation of N_T, which are usually unknown. Thirdly, the relation between $\log N_{T+1}$ and $\log N_T$ may not be truly linear. The worst objection is that any constant trend, upwards or downwards, in the values of $\log N_T$ will tend to make $b = 1$. It is quite easy to visualize why that should be, or alternatively, the effect may be proved algebraically. Cyclic behaviour, i.e. a series of upward and downward trends, may also bias the value of b (Southwood 1967). So the existence of consistent trends or cycles makes the estimation of density dependence very hazardous, partly for technical reasons, but partly because we must then define precisely what we mean by density-dependence in such situations. The notion of density dependence implies the existence of a norm, which might be a long-term average, or a steady trend or cycle. Only when we have arbitrarily specified what kind of norm the population has, can we examine deviations from the norm. Indeed, the only valid definition of true cyclicity in animal populations is a tendency to overshoot past a norm (Moran 1952). Perhaps the most devastating criticism of all is not technical but biological. Many biologists are unimpressed by demonstrations that density dependence exists when the biological mechanism is unknown. The analysis is sometimes done because somebody has collected a series of estimates of N_T, and cannot think what else to do with them.

Similar technical problems beset attempts to show that reproduction is density dependent. The ratio of the number of progeny to the number of adults may well decrease as the number of adults increases, but that is to be expected statistically, because 'number of adults' is used to calculate the ratio. The usual significance tests, which assume that the remainders are statistically independent, cannot be used. That does not mean that an observed biological effect of this kind is necessarily bogus.

Much more ambitious are attempts to investigate the biological processes which determine the size of an animal population. The old idea that 'all animals are equal' has long since disappeared. Two populations of the same size but different age-structure show very different rates of change. (This makes the value of the theoretical concept of 'intrinsic rate of increase' very doubtful, because the intrinsic rate postulates the existence of an ideal age-structure which may never be achieved in practice. There is no reason to suppose that a high intrinsic rate of increase is intrinsically beneficial, except perhaps to colonizing or ephemeral species.) So a detailed analysis of population processes must recognize different age-classes of animal, and therefore use 'life tables'. It is not unusual for males and females to behave differently, and so the analysis must distinguish between the sexes. In real life, birth- and survival-rates vary with time, as well as with age and sex. The study of population dynamics therefore uses computer models which apply appropriate birth- and survival-rates to male and female life tables. Ecological work on rabbits, fish, and birds has shown the importance of the social status of individual animals, but the benefits of that social status have rarely been measured. Rates of immigration and emigration and of gene flow are usually unknown, yet they actually define what we mean by 'an animal population'. These, and other relevant complications, all ought to be included in a population study. Computer simulation models can certainly make allowance for all these effects, once the biology is known, but simulation models lie outside the scope of this book.

Finally, let us consider the distinction between deterministic and stochastic theory. If ducks lay, on average, 4·6 eggs each, the deterministic theory says that each individual duck shall lay exactly 4·6 eggs. The stochastic theory takes the more reasonable view that different individuals may lay 1, 2, 3, 4, 5 . . . eggs. The stochastic theory therefore requires more information than the deterministic. It has to know, not just the average number of eggs, but the distribution of eggs per individual. A duck which lays six eggs is likely to have many more grandchildren than a duck which lays only one egg. So, in the stochastic theory of populations, the variability of the different possible outcomes builds up from generation to generation. In other words, starting from a given situation, our predictions of the outcome must become more and more uncertain as time goes on. At the price of requiring the extra information, a stochastic theory will predict the variability to be expected after several generations, whereas the deterministic theory can only predict an average population size. If the various biological processes which determine the numbers of animals are inter-related *linearly*, the deterministic answer must equal the average stochastic answer. But, in biology, relations are not often linear, and so it is theoretically possible that the deterministic answer is far removed from the true average. There is not yet enough evidence to decide whether that is often true in real cases, but it is observed that animal numbers generally fluctuate much less than might be expected from those animals' observed powers of increase. Natural stochastic variations are generally small, and so we may reasonably expect the deterministic answer to be fairly representative, in most real cases.

Stochastic theory (e.g. Bartlett 1960) can provide insight which the deterministic theory completely misses. Consider a closed animal population with equal birth- and death-rates. (*Every* surviving population must, in the long run, have approximately equal birth- and death-rates.) The deterministic theory says that the population numbers will remain constant, because births exactly balance deaths. The stochastic theory says that the probability of extinction will steadily increase as time goes on, so that any such population can be expected to go extinct at some finite time in the future — there is no chance that it will survive *ad infinitum*. It is easy to see why. At every generation, there must be some probability (even if small) that the population vanishes, and once that has happened, the population cannot re-establish itself. So extinction is an inescapable trap which always lies in wait. If we started with a whole set of such populations, we should find that after some time a lot had gone extinct, but a few had waxed and multiplied. The stochastic average would agree with the deterministic steady-state, but the stochastic distribution of possible outcomes would be very skew, in favour of zero. Extinction is still inevitable, even when the birth- and death- rates are density dependent. It is a fallacy to suppose that density dependence can save a population from extinction in the long run. No ecological system can be perfectly stable — we have to think in terms of relative stabilities. But, with density-dependent survival, a population will take very much longer (on average) to go extinct than the same population with density-independent survival. Therefore, stochastic theory tells us that the crux of the argument about density dependence is, 'How long do real live populations take, on average, to go extinct?' — which, of course, we do not know.

This chapter has discussed the limitations of some purely statistical methods of analysing population data. In the study of animal populations, these 'orthodox' statistical methods are now giving place to computer simulation models, which (properly used) can give a much more dynamic, and therefore realistic, picture of the biological events. Such models, although still in their infancy, would need a whole book to themselves.

Example 11

(1) Verify, from the formula for calculating a regression coefficient (Chap. 3), that if the regression of y on x is b, the regression coefficient of $(y - x)$ on x is $b - 1$. In other words, that we get the same answer if we (a) predict the value of y and then subtract x, or (b) predict $(y - x)$ directly from x.

12 | A WARNING

THIS book treats statistical analyses as tools. If the biological answer is already obvious, there is no need to do the analysis. But that utilitarian point of view does not excuse sloppiness. The tools must be used carefully. It is no use doing an analysis, if you do not do it correctly. Fortunately, computers make many fewer arithmetic mistakes than do humans. But if the data are wrong, the answer will be wrong. Using computers, we do not get the same intimate acquaintance with the data that we get when using desk calculators, and so we should check the data very carefully, and then use the data checks which are (or should be) built into the program. Some people argue that, since the original data are subject to errors of measurement, there is no need to worry if further errors are introduced during the analysis. That careless attitude leads to trouble. The extra errors will inflate the 'residual' mean square, so reducing the apparent accuracy of the results. And once the data checks have been compromised, there can be no assurance about the magnitude of the new errors — they may seriously affect the estimates of means or regressions. Every analysis must be done rigorously; for example, if we decide to predict y from x by a straight line, we should use regression analysis. Lines drawn by eye often differ surprisingly from the true regression line; after all, there are *two* distinct regression lines, namely y on x and x on y (Chap. 3). Inefficient methods of analysis sometimes give answers which the data, treated properly, actually contradict. So if an analysis is superfluous, do not do it; but if it is necessary, do it well.

13 | CURVE-FITTING

S O far, we have been dealing mainly with linear models (Chap. 4), but, in biology, straight lines are rather rare. Very often, a simple transformation will convert a curve to something that, for practical purposes, is near enough a straight line (Example 1, Chap. 3). There is a good reason for using linear methods, wherever possible. In many areas of applied mathematics — e.g. control theory, econometrics, and thermodynamics — the theory is very strong for linear applications and painfully weak for non-linear; statistics is no exception. It is certainly possible to study particular types of curves, e.g. exponentials or polynomials, in some detail, but the class of 'all possible non-linear curves' is too broad to permit anything but vague theoretical generalizations. Yet, sometimes, we do need to fit a curve to a set of data, where no obvious transformation to linearity exists. Such problems do not occur very often in everyday statistical analysis, but nowadays they arise very frequently when we make computer simulation models. We shall not discuss, here, the construction and use of simulation models as such, but this chapter will consider curve-fitting in general. The problem is this: given a set of data, we wish to fit a curve to predict appropriate values of y from the corresponding values of x. Usually, there is no theoretical reason to prefer any particular type of curve. So the problem has two parts: first, to choose a suitable type of curve, and second, to estimate the appropriate parameters.

In the past, many statisticians have used 'smoothing' techniques to remove accidental irregularities from the data. Nowadays, such techniques are little used in biology, because there is no reliable way of distinguishing genuine biological effects from the accidental irregularities. Here, we are not merely 'smoothing', but choosing an appropriate type of mathematical function and fitting its parameters to the data.

There are no rules for choosing curves. Choice of an appropriate formula is largely a matter of experience. Where the data show a steady (even though non-linear) progression (as in Fig. 13.1(a)) it is usually quite easy to find a suitable form of curve to fit them. Indeed, it is often quite easy to find several different curves, and different mathematicians tend to favour different types of curve. Provided there is no theoretical reason to prefer one over another, and provided we do not want to extrapolate along the curve beyond the range of observations, any one of those curves may be adopted. For example, in Fig. 13.1(a),

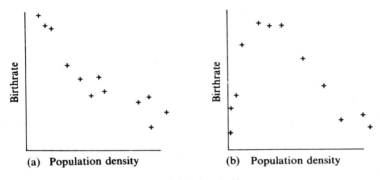

(a) **Population density** (b) **Population density**

Fig. 13.1. (a) and (b).

we might try an exponential $y = a + \exp\left[c(b - x)\right]$, a parabola $y = a + c(x - b)^2$, or a hyperbola $y = a + c/(x - b)$. Incidentally, all those formulae have three parameters a, b, and c. Their actual values would be very different in each case, but they would still be doing the same jobs: a and b serving to locate the scales of y and x, while c determines the amount of curvature. The three formulae might all fit equally well, but they would diverge sharply outside the range of observations shown in Fig. 13.1(a). Now it would be quite easy to find a transformation (perhaps the mathematical equivalent of one of these same formulae) to convert Fig. 13.1(a) to a straight line. But sometimes the data follow a more tortuous path, as in Fig. 13.1(b). We can then try to find a composite formula whose different parts will take care of different parts of the curve. At the righthand side of Fig. 13.1(b), the values of y seem to be declining gradually towards zero, which suggests an exponential decline, $y = e^{-bx}$. The initial rise of y might then be represented by a power of x, $y = x^a$, or perhaps by a positive exponential, $y = e^{ax} - 1$ (the value 1 is subtracted because y has to be 0 when $x = 0$). Putting the parts together, we might try $y = cx^a e^{-bx}$ or $y = c(e^{-ax} - e^{-bx})$; the first formula is rather easier to

Curve Fitting

fit (Example 1, this chapter). There is, of course, no guarantee that either formula shall fit a given set of data satisfactorily. Watt (1961) gives a useful key to different types of equation, which is reprinted by Southwood (1966). Although Watt's curves are quoted as differential equations, they can all be solved to give an explicit relation between y and x. If no suitable formula for a curve can be found, it is always possible to fit a polynomial (Chap. 4) — and, indeed, a quadratic or cubic polynomial is often a very suitable choice. However, a polynomial, if it is to fit a rather tortuous curve like Fig. 13.1(b), must include many more coefficients than the three (a, b, and c) of $y = cx^a e^{-bx}$; so 'analytic' functions of the latter type, where applicable, are to be preferred, partly for their mathematical elegance, but mainly because of the dangers of extrapolation, mentioned in the next paragraph. Finally, it is always possible to avoid the problem of curve-fitting by tabulating a series of values of y, and interpolating between them. There are various methods of interpolation, but each is equivalent to fitting a particular type (linear, quadratic, etc.) of curve to a small local region of the whole curve. Interpolation is evidently not very satisfactory when the data points jump about, as in Fig. 13.1.

Chapter 4 mentioned the dangers of extrapolating outside the range of the data. But we may be fitting a curve because we want to use it in a simulation model, and, once that simulation model is made, we shall start asking, 'What would happen if . . . ?' In other words, we shall present new, hypothetical situations to the model. Very often, those hypothetical situations are simply new assortments within the observed range of parameters, but sometimes they involve some extrapolation beyond that range. Extrapolations a short distance beyond the range may reasonably be accepted, but the grosser the extrapolation, the more sceptical we must be. Since violent discontinuities are rather unusual in biology, we can usually trust a smooth curve better than one which bends itself in knots. The dangers of extrapolation are always with us, but they are especially great in a high-order polynomial, which sometimes bends about in an artificial — and very disconcerting — way, immediately outside the range of the data to which it has been fitted. That is why polynomials of order higher than quadratic or cubic are best avoided — except as a last resort.

Once we have chosen a suitable type of curve, we have to find appropriate values of its parameters to suit the data. Sometimes it is possible to transform to linearity, and use linear regression (Example 1, this chapter). Sometimes no such transformation exists, in which case we can use non-linear regression (Chap. 4), or its equivalent, trial-and-error linear regression. Computer programs for non-linear regression work on the same trial-and-error principles as are used in Example 2 of this chapter, but they work automatically, so that the user has no control over the operation. Now, as Example 2 shows, a method which pays too much attention to one particular part of the curve may leave another part unconsidered. Once a curve has been fitted (by whatever method), therefore, it must always be plotted against the original data, partly to see if the mathematical formula is appropriate in the first place, and partly to make sure that the fit is everywhere good. In some cases, an automatic non-linear regression program will not achieve convergence, i.e. it will not produce one definite answer. That may mean that it is being asked to fit a wildly inappropriate curve to the data, but it may merely mean that the particular program cannot cope adequately with the particular set of data. Such ambiguities do not arise when we ourselves control the curve-fitting operation, as in Example 2.

It is tempting, once a formula has been found, to interpret its terms biologically: 'this term must represent such-and-such a biological process, while that one . . .'. But it is very dangerous to do this, unless the particular type of formula was chosen *a priori* for theoretical reasons. If a set of data conforms to some curve, we cannot deduce the underlying biology with any certainty, any more than we can deduce underlying biology from an observed distribution (Chap. 9). On the other hand, if we observe that (say) $y = ae^{kt}$, we can at least assert that y obeys the equation $dy/dt = ky$, even if we do not understand why.

Examples 13

(1) To fit a curve to the net number of eggs produced per day by a population of insects as a function of population density.

Number of eggs (y)	4	14	23	35	24	15	9	2	2
Density (x)	20	48	87	210	280	410	500	600	700

The plot of y against x looks rather like Fig. 13.1(b).
(a) The curve is very skew. The logarithmic transformation expands the lower part of the scale of measurement (Chap. 5), and so the plot of y against $\log x$ might be shaped like a Normal probability curve, in which case y will be proportional to $\exp[a(\log x - m)^2]$ for some values of a and m. We can turn this into a linear relation by writing $\log y = a(\log x)^2 + b(\log x) + c$. Find a, b, and c by multiple regression of $\log y$ on $\log x$ and $(\log x)^2$, using natural logarithms for comparison with (b).

Curve Fitting

(b) As stated in the text, $y = cx^a e^{-bx}$ might be suitable. When x is near zero, e^{-bx} is nearly 1, and the curve is dominated by x^a. When x is large, the exponential far outweighs x^a in importance. If $y = c x^a e^{-bx}$, the relation is made linear by $\log y = \log c + a \log x - bx$, (using natural logarithms). Find a, b, and c by multiple regression of $\log y$ on $\log x$ and x. Try plotting $y = cx^a$, $y = e^{-bx}$, and $y = cx^a e^{-bx}$. Is (a) or (b) preferable, in this case?

(2) An exercise in curve-fitting by non-linear regression.

The data of Example 1 (Chap. 3) show exponential growth which seems to slow down towards the end. The equation for pure exponential growth is $dN/dt = rN$ (Watt's curve A-24) (Watt 1961). We may, therefore, try $dN/dt = rN(A - N)$ where A is an asymptote; as N approaches A, the rate of growth declines. This is Watt's equation A-22. Its solution takes the form $N = 1/(a + be^{-kt})$. This is a sigmoid curve which starts at $N = 1/(a + b)$, when $t = 0$, and climbs towards the asymptote $N = 1/a$, as t tends to infinity. In this example, the values of N are generally large, and it is convenient for reasons of scale to use the equivalent $N = 100/(a + be^{-kt})$.

(a) If $N = 100/(a + be^{-kt})$, it follows that $100/N = a + be^{-kt}$, i.e. the regression of $100/N$ on e^{-kt} should be linear for some value of k. Form a new variate $y = 100/N$ and new variates $x = e^{-kt}$ for trial values of $k = 0.0115$, 0.012, 0.0125, 0.013, and 0.135. Regress y on each of the xs, and show that the correlation between x and y is greatest when $k = 0.0125$. From the corresponding regression equation, deduce a formula for N in terms of t. Plot the data and the fitted curve. This formula gives a very bad representation of the growth curve, because the transformation $x = e^{-kt}$ makes the small values of t overwhelmingly important, at the expense of later values.

(b) If $N = 100/(a + be^{-kt})$, it follows that $\log(100/N - a)$ should be a linear function of t, for some value of a. If the growth curve is purely exponential $a = 0$. Form new variates $y = \log(100/N - a)$ for trial values of $a = 0.003$, 0.004, 0.005, 0.006, and 0.007. Regress each y on t, and show that the correlation between y and t is greatest when $a = 0.005$. From the corresponding regression equation, deduce a formula for N in terms of t. Plot the data and the fitted curve. This formula gives an acceptable representation of the growth curve, because the regression of y on t pays equal attention to all values of t. However, the formula takes no fewer than three parameters to represent only ten original data points, and it is still doubtful whether a differs from zero, i.e. whether the growth curve is not exponential.

(3) Some standard types of curve.

(a) The exponential, $y = e^{kx}$ (Watt's A-24 and A-30) (Watt 1961). Plot the four curves corresponding to $k = 2, 1, -1$, and -2 for values of $x = 0, 1, 2, 3, 5, 10$. What happens if $k = 0$?

(b) The power, $y = x^a$ (Watt's A-20). Plot the four curves corresponding to $a = \frac{1}{2}, 1, 1\frac{1}{2}$, and 2 for values of $x = 0, 1, 2, 3, 5, 10$. If $a \leqslant 1$, the curve rises directly from the origin; if $a > 1$, it touches the x-axis at the origin. What happens when $x < 0$ if a is (i) even, (ii) odd, and (iii) a fraction?

(c) The sigmoid — Example 2.

(d) The logarithm (Watt's A-28 and A-31) — Example 1 (Chap. 5).

14 OUTLINE OF METHODS

T H I S chapter sketches the process used to tackle any particular problem. The final chapter of Hald's book (1952) (see references) gives a rather theoretical account of the same process, while Bailey's (1959) summary tells how to choose an appropriate method of analysis. The following outline does not imply that biological research can be done by rote.

(1) First specify, as explicitly as possible, the biological questions to be asked (Chap. 8). This does not mean that you cannot consider other questions which may suggest themselves later (Chap. 2).

(2) If relevant data do not already exist, choose the appropriate methods of experimentation or observation. The criteria are relevance (the biological effect under examination must not be confounded with other, unwanted effects – Chap. 8), efficiency (the greatest accuracy at least cost), and practical convenience. Consider how big a sample is needed to give the desired accuracy (Chap. 8). Sometimes, it is impossible, or impracticable, to answer the chosen biological questions, in which case, return to point (1). This book does not consider complicated experimental design, which is a job for an expert.

(3) The method of analysis of the data will depend on the choice of an underlying statistical model (Chap. 4). We usually use standard methods of analysis which depend on standard models of additive effects and linear regressions (Chaps. 2, 3 and 4). It is often possible to transform data to satisfy those models, at least approximately (Chap. 5). The model used to analyse a complicated experiment will correspond to the design of that experiment. Consider how you will analyse the data, *before* you take the observations.

(4) The analysis will usually involve estimation of some parameters (e.g. means or regression coefficients) by least squares (Chap. 1) or maximum likelihood (Chap. 7).

(5) Use the estimated values to see if the model agrees well enough with the data. This may be done graphically (Chap. 3), or by a special

goodness-of-fit test, but it is often not necessary to examine the agreement very closely, because we rely on the robustness (Chap. 4) of ordinary statistical methods.

(6) Consider whether the biological story, which the statistics tell, makes sense. (If not, *either* you have done something wrong *or* you are on the trail of a momentous discovery.) Consider the size of the biological effects observed, to see if they are worth bothering about. If the story is worth pursuing, return to point (1).

If you are in doubt about the suitability of a proposed method of analysis to answer some chosen question, simply translate that analysis into its underlying model (Chap. 4) and distribution of remainders. It will then be easy to decide whether the analysis is suitable. The commonest type of analysis examines the means of one or more samples, usually *via* an analysis of variance. The variance-ratio (F-) test can be used to compare several means; that same test, or the equivalent t-test, can compare two means, or one mean and its theoretical value (Chap. 2). If the data are whole-number counts, they may need transformation (Chaps. 5 and 11). A transformation may also be advisable for data which can vary continuously, e.g. direct measurements or percentages, but, quite often, the standard assumptions of additive treatment effects and approximately Normal residuals are adequate. Two-way tables should be made orthogonal whenever possible, because non-orthogonal tables are difficult to interpret (Chap. 2). The next most common type of analysis examines the relation between two or more variates. Correlation measures the strength of the association, i.e. the degree to which one variate may be predicted from another, while regression gives the actual prediction formula (Chap. 3). Both correlation and regression assume linearity. Multiple regressions may be difficult to interpret, and in any case, regressions never prove causality (Chap. 3). Only deliberately designed experiments can prove causality (Chap. 8). The analysis of experimental results is dictated by the design of the experiment, i.e. the analysis examines those questions which are built into the experiment. Values of χ^2 calculated from contingency tables and from other sets of counts are really weighted sums of squares (Chap. 1). Before we compare a calculated value of χ^2 with its theoretical (tabulated) value, we must make sure that underlying assumptions are justified (Chap. 6). Analyses are done to answer biological questions, and so the answers must always make biological sense.

REFERENCES

Allard, R. W., Babbel, G. R., Clegg, M. T., and Kahler, A. L. (1972). Evidence of coadaption in *Avena barbata*. *Proc. natn Acad. Sci.* **69**, 3043.

Bailey, N. T. J. (1959). *Statistical methods in biology*. E.U.P., London.

Bailey, N. T. J. (1967). *The mathematical approach to biology and medicine*. Wiley, New York.

Bartlett, M. S. (1960). *Stochastic population models in ecology and epidemiology*. Methuen, London.

Cochran, W. G. and Cox, G. M. (1957). *Experimental designs*. Wiley, New York.

Falconer, D. S. (1961). *Introduction to quantitative genetics*. Oliver and Boyd, Edinburgh.

Fisher, R. A. (1918). The correlation between relatives on the supposition of Mendelian inheritance. *Trans. R. Soc. Edin.* **52**, 399.

Fisher, R. A. (1959). *Statistical methods and scientific inference*. Oliver and Boyd, Edinburgh.

Fisher, R. A. and Yates, F. (1953). *Statistical tables for biological, agricultural and medical research*. Oliver and Boyd, Edinburgh.

Gilbert, N. (1961a). Polygene analysis. *Genet. Res.* **2**, 456.

Gilbert, N. (1961b). Quantitative inheritance in *Drosophila*. *J. Genet.* **57**, 77.

Gilbert, N. (1967). Additive combining abilities fitted to plant breeding data. *Biometrics*. **23**, 45.

Greig-Smith, P. (1964). *Quantitative plant ecology*. Butterworths, London.

Hald, A. (1952). *Statistical theory with engineering applications*. Wiley, New York.

Healy, M. J. R. (1963). Fitting a quadratic. *Biometrics* **19**, 362.

Jeffreys, H. (1939). *Theory of probability*. Clarendon Press, Oxford.

Kendall, M. G. and Stuart, A. (1963). *The advanced theory of statistics*. Griffin, London.

Moll, R. H. and Robinson, H. F. (1966). Observed and expected response in four experiments in maize. *Crop Sci.* **6**, 319.

Moran, P. A. P. (1952). The statistical analysis of game-bird records. *J. Anim. Ecol.* **21**, 154.

Morris, R. F. (1953). Single factor analysis in population dynamics. *Ecology* **40**, 580.

Penny, L. H., Russell, W. A., Sprague, G. F. and Hallauer, A. R. (1963). Recurrent selection, in *Statistical genetics and plant breeding*. U.S. natn Acad. Sci.

Sheldon, B. L. (1963). Studies in artificial selection of quantitative characters. *Aust. J. biol. Sci.* **16**, 490.

Southwood, T. R. E. (1966). *Ecological methods*. Methuen, London.

Southwood, T. R. E. (1967). The interpretation of population change. *J. Anim. Ecol.* **36**, 519.

Sprent, P. (1970). Some problems of statistical consultancy. *J. R. Stat. Soc. A*. **133**, 139.

Spickett, S. G. and Thoday, J. M. (1966). Regular responses to selection. Interaction between located polygenes. *Genet. Res.* **7**, 96.

Tukey, J. W. (1949). One degree of freedom for non-additivity. *Biometrics* **5**, 232.

Tukey, J. W. (1954). Causation, regression and path analysis. in *Statistics and mathematics in biology* (ed. O. Kempthorne). Iowa State College Press.

Varley, G. C. and Gradwell, G. R. (1960). Key factors in population studies. *J. Anim. Ecol.* **29**, 399.

Watt, K. E. F. (1961). Mathematical models for use in insect pest control. *Can. Ent.* **93**, suppl. 19.

Williams, C. B. (1964). *Patterns in the balance of nature*. Academic Press, New York.

Yates, F. (1947). The analysis of data from all possible reciprocal crosses between a set of parental lines. *Heredity* **1**, 287.

Yates, F. (1955). A note on the application of the combination of probabilities test to a set of 2 x 2 tables. *Biometrika* **42**, 404.

ANSWERS TO EXAMPLES

Chapter 1

Example 2

(a) By calculus: differentiating $\Sigma(y - m)^2$ with regard to m,
$\Sigma(y - m) = 0$, i.e. $m = \bar{y}$.
(b) By algebra: let $m = \bar{y} + a$, say,

$$\text{then } \Sigma(y - m)^2 = \Sigma(y - \bar{y} - a)^2$$
$$= \Sigma[(y - \bar{y})^2 - 2a(y - \bar{y}) + a^2]$$
$$= \Sigma(y - \bar{y})^2 + Na^2 \text{, since } \Sigma(y - \bar{y}) = 0.$$

Therefore $\Sigma(y - m)^2$ is least when $a = 0$, i.e. when $m = \bar{y}$.

Example 3

$$\Sigma(y - \bar{y})^2 = \Sigma(y^2 - 2\bar{y}y + \bar{y}^2)$$
$$= \Sigma y^2 - 2\bar{y}\Sigma y + N\bar{y}^2$$
$$= \Sigma y^2 - 2\bar{y}(N\bar{y}) + N\bar{y}^2$$
$$= \Sigma y^2 - N\bar{y}^2.$$

Chapter 2

Example 1

Analysis of variance

	Degrees of freedom	Mean square
Between sexes	1	172·8
Residual	6	1·2

It would be possible, instead, to treat males and females quite separately.

	Degrees of freedom	Sum of squares	Mean square
Variance of males	4	5·2	1·3
Variance of females	2	2·0	1·0

Unless there is reason to suppose that males are intrinsically more variable than females (or vice versa), we combine the two estimates of variance to obtain greater accuracy (more degrees of freedom). Then the combined sum of squares 5·2 + 2·0 has 4 + 2 degrees of freedom, giving the mean square 1·2 (with 6 degrees of freedom) which appears in the analysis of variance. This mean square is used to calculate the following variances, on the assumption that in future we shall always distinguish males from females, and allow for the difference between them. By taking the trouble to distinguish the two sexes, we eliminate that part of the over-all variability, which arises from the difference male versus female.

Mean of males	38·6 with variance	0·24
Mean of females	29·0	0·40
Over-all mean	35·0	0·15
Average of male, female means	33·8	0·16
Difference between male, female means	9·6	0·64

The 'average of male, female means' has greater variance, i.e. is less accurate than, the over-all mean. That must always be so, unless the sample numbers of males and females are the same. But there is evidently a real difference in length between males and females. Therefore, the over-all mean composed of 5 males: 3 females is rather meaningless. It estimates the mean of 'all possible samples, or populations, which happen to contain a 5:3 sex ratio'. The 'average of male, female means', on the other hand, estimates the mean of all samples, or a whole population, with a 1:1 sex ratio.

Example 2

The value 4·37 is obviously wrong. No pig can grow 4 cm per day, even for one day. If we use nonsensical data, the answer will be nonsense.

(a) If we omit the value 4·37 altogether, we obtain the analysis of variance as follows.

	Degrees of freedom	Mean square
Between lots	2	0·10326
Residual	10	0·00410

$$m_1 = 1·08 \text{ with standard error } 0·032,$$
$$m_2 = 1·28 \qquad 0·032,$$
$$m_3 = 1·38 \qquad 0·029,$$
$$m_2 - m_1 = 0·20 \qquad 0·045,$$
$$m_3 - m_2 = 0·10 \qquad 0·043,$$
$$m_3 - \tfrac{1}{2}m_1 - \tfrac{1}{2}m_2 = 0·20 \qquad 0·036.$$

Answers

(b) If we assume that 4·37 is a misrecording of 1·37, and substitute that value we obtain the analysis of variance as follows.

	Degrees of freedom	Mean square
Between lots	2	0·10889
Remainder	11	0·00374

$$m_1 = 1·08 \text{ with standard error } 0·031,$$
$$m_2 = 1·28 \qquad\qquad 0·031,$$
$$m_3 = 1·38 \qquad\qquad 0·025,$$
$$m_2 - m_1 = 0·20 \qquad\qquad 0·043,$$
$$m_3 - m_2 = 0·10 \qquad\qquad 0·039,$$
$$m_3 - \tfrac{1}{2}m_1 - \tfrac{1}{2}m_2 = 0·20 \qquad\qquad 0·033.$$

The genetical conclusions are the same in both cases. The comparison $m_2 - m_1$ shows that Landrace pigs grow rather faster than Large White, and the other two comparisons show that the hybrids grow faster than the parental average, but not significantly faster than the best parent.
(c) If the deviant value 4·37 is retained, m_3 becomes 1·88, but the 'residual' mean square increases to 0·6801. The mean changes by 36 per cent, but the mean square by 16 488 per cent. This shows that the variance is very much less robust than the mean (Chap. 4).

Example 3

Analysis of variance

	Degrees of freedom	Mean square
Between treatments	1	4·8000
Between nests within treatments	8	0·4743
Between chicks within nests	20	0·1280

Why are there not 9 degrees of freedom between the ten nests? — because one of those degrees of freedom has already been accounted for, as the difference between treatments. After *two* 'treatments' means have been fitted to *ten* nests, there are only 8 degrees of freedom left between nests — 4 degrees of freedom between five 'control' nests, and 4 between five 'extra food' nests.

The chicks given extra food *on average* gained more weight (how much?). The treatment 'extra food' is given to whole nests, not to individual chicks in a nest. The nest is the experimental unit; the comparison between treatments is a comparison between two sets of *nests*. So if extra food had no effect, we should expect the 'between treatments' mean square to be the same as the 'between nests' mean square.

Therefore, to test the significance of treatment differences, we must use the 'between nests' mean square as residual, not the 'between chicks within nests' mean square. The point is further discussed in Chapter 6. If the 'between nests' mean square had turned out to be the same size as the 'between chicks' mean square, we could assume that there were no consistent differences between nests (within any one treatment), i.e. that 'between nests' mean square and 'between chicks' mean square were estimating the same residual variance. It would then be valid to calculate a combined residual, with 28 degrees of freedom. In this case, 0·4743 is considerably (even if not significantly) bigger than 0·1280, and so the two mean squares should not be combined. Therefore, to compare the two treatments, we could just as well have recorded nest totals, rather than individual chicks, because the nest is the relevant experimental unit.

Example 4

Analysis of variance

	Degrees of freedom	Mean square
Between sexes	1	24·50
Between species	2	328·22
Interaction	2	48·67
Remainder	12	5·67

The variance ratio 24·50/5·67 shows that males are faster than females on average, but the variance ratio 48·67/5·67 shows that the difference varies from species to species. The original data show that male kangaroos are considerably faster than females, but the two sexes of cheetah and greyhound are about equally fast. That is reasonable, because female kangaroos are almost always carrying young. Cheetahs are faster than kangaroos, which are faster than greyhounds (by how much?).

Example 5

(a)

Analysis of variance

	Degrees of freedom	Mean square
Between nationalities	2	19·29
Residual	15	5·09

Australians apparently drink more than the others.

Answers

(b) Analysis of variance

	Degrees of freedom	Mean square
Nationalities	2	19·29
Sexes (adj. nationalities)	1	58·43
Nationalities (adj. sexes)	2	0·31
Sexes	1	96·39
Interaction	1	0·14
Remainder	13	1·37

The 'nationalities' mean square is necessarily the same as in (a). 'Nationalities (adj. sexes)' mean square is insignificant, and so the apparent differences between nationalities may be ascribed to the fact that all the Australians were male. Inspection of the data shows that the interpretation is reasonable. Why is there only one degree of freedom for 'interaction'?

Example 6

'Columns adj. rows' mean square must also be large. There are real differences between columns. 'Rows adj. columns' mean square is large, so there are some real differences between rows, which by chance cancel out when mixed with the indirect columns effects in the 'rows' mean square.

Example 7

The 'residual' sum of squares, minimized by fitting both row- and column-constants, cannot exceed the 'residual' sum of squares, minimized by fitting row-constants only. Therefore, the sum of squares *accounted for* cannot be less.

Example 8

By definition, V = average of $(y - m)^2$

$$= \mathrm{av}(y^2 - 2\,my + m^2) = \mathrm{av}(y^2) - m^2.$$

Therefore, $\mathrm{av}(y^2) = m^2 + V$.

Similarly, $\mathrm{av}(\bar{y}^2) = m^2 + V/N$, since the mean and variance of $\bar{y}$ are m and V/N.

Therefore,

$$\mathrm{av}(\Sigma(y - \bar{y})^2) = \mathrm{av}(\Sigma y^2 - N\bar{y}^2)$$

$$= N\,\mathrm{av}(y^2) - N\,\mathrm{av}(\bar{y}^2)$$

$$= N(m^2 + V - m^2 - V/N) = (N - 1)V.$$

Example 10

Weighted $\bar{y} = \Sigma a_i y_i$, where $a_i = w_i/\Sigma w_i$.

Its variance $= \Sigma a_i^2 V_i$, which reduces to $1/\Sigma w_i$, since $V_i = 1/w_i$.

118

Chapter 3

Example 1
(a) Count = $-2426 + 29 \cdot 2$ (time), a significant regression, but a poor fit.
(b) Log_e (count) = $3 \cdot 511 + 0 \cdot 0152$ (time), a much better representation but perhaps still not perfect. The growth of bacteria was exponential for 300 minutes, but thereafter seems to slow down (see Chap. 13, Example 2).

Example 2
The regressions are the same for adult males and females, and so those two categories may be combined. Then the regression of weight on distance for adults is

$$\text{weight} = 4 \cdot 06 - 0 \cdot 0026 \text{ (distance)},$$

giving predictions of $2 \cdot 8$ g and $-1 \cdot 1$ g at 500 miles and 2000 miles. The negative figure is an extrapolation outside the range of the observations, and shows that the bird could not fly 2000 miles non-stop. The regression of distance on weight for juveniles is

$$\text{distance} = 1194 - 232 \text{ (weight)},$$

giving a prediction of 730 miles flown by a bird weighing $2 \cdot 0$ g.

Example 3
Last part first: If V is the variance of individual values of y, the mean of y in block 1 is $\bar{y}_1 = \sum_1 y/N_1$ with variance V/N_1 and, therefore, with weight $w_1 = N_1/V$. Similarly, for the second block. The weighted mean is $(w_1 \bar{y}_1 + w_2 \bar{y}_2)/(w_1 + w_2)$ which, on substituting the values of w and $\bar{y}$, becomes $(\sum_1 y + \sum_2 y)/(N_1 + N_2)$. So the weighted mean, which is the most accurate combination of the two block means, equals the over-all mean. A similar argument is used in the first part of the question, where $b_1 = \sum_1 (y - \bar{y}_1)(x - \bar{x}_1)/\sum_1 (x - \bar{x}_1)^2$, with variance $V/\sum_1 (x - \bar{x}_1)^2$.

Example 4
$x_1 = 1$ for Large Whites and 0, otherwise; $x_2 = 1$ for Landrace and 0, otherwise. Then the regression of growth rate on the dummy variates is $y = 1 \cdot 382 - 0 \cdot 302 x_1 - 0 \cdot 097 x_2$, giving $\bar{y} = 1 \cdot 080$ for Large White $(x_1 = 1, x_2 = 0)$; $y = 1 \cdot 285$ for Landrace $(x_1 = 0, x_2 = 1)$; and $y = 1 \cdot 382$ for the cross $(x_1 = x_2 = 0)$. The analysis of variance for the regression is identical with that for the one-way analysis.
Regression on the single dummy variate would absorb only one degree of freedom, and would require that $\bar{y} = a + 2b$ for the cross,

Answers

$\bar{y} = a + b$ for Landrace, and $\bar{y} = a$ for Large White; i.e. it would arbitrarily require that the difference between Landrace and Large White must equal that between the cross and Landrace.

Example 5

The single regression of 'number of babies' on calendar year leaves a 'residual' mean square 28 595 (11 degrees of freedom). The multiple regression on years and nests leaves a 'residual' mean square 28 422 (10 degrees of freedom). The reduction is negligible, and certainly not significant (variance ratio = 30 326/28 422 with 1 and 10 degrees of freedom).

Example 6

(a) Correlation between fleas and fish = 0·686 (6 degrees of freedom). The data prove neither assertion.
(b) Correlation between cat's weight and fish = 0·288 (6 degrees of freedom), between cat's weight and fleas = −0·394 (6 degrees of freedom). Alternatively, and equivalently, the single regressions of cat's weight on fish and on fleas are not significantly great.
(c) The multiple regression of cat's weight on fish and fleas gives a variance ratio ('regression' mean square/'residual' mean square) of 7·26 with 2 and 5 degrees of freedom.

Example 7

(b) The regression equation $y = a + b_1(x_1 + x_3) + b_2(x_1 - x_3)$ is identical with $y = a + (b_1 + b_2)x_1 + (b_1 - b_2)x_3$. Therefore, a multiple regression on $(x_1 + x_3)$ and $(x_1 - x_3)$ must always give the same predictions as — and its coefficients can be deduced from — the multiple regression on x_1 and x_3. Similarly, (d) $y = a + b(x_1 + x_2 + x_3)$ is the same as $y = a + 3b(x_1 + x_2 + x_3)/3$, i.e. the regressions on $x_1 + x_2 + x_3$ and on $(x_1 + x_2 + x_3)/3$ are equivalent, and one coefficient is three times the other.

Chapter 4

Example 2

In an extreme case, suppose that x_1 always equals x_2, and that the regression of y on x_1 is $y = a + bx_1$. Then the multiple regression of y on x_1 and x_2, i.e. on the same x-variate twice, must give precisely the same predictions, and may be written $y = a + gx_1 + (b - g)x_2$, where g can take any value we please. For whatever g may be, this equation reduces to $y = a + bx$. So the multiple-regression coefficients are indeterminate, but the predictions are the same whatever g may be. The coefficients actually calculated by the computer, will depend on how the program does the calculations. In this example, the two x-variates are very highly (but not completely) correlated. The multiple-regression coefficients are unstable, and their standard errors are therefore very large, compared with the standard errors of the corresponding single-regression coefficients.

Chapter 5

Example 3

All three plots are approximately linear. If any transformation is used at all, (c) is preferable because the scatter of y about the regression line remains the same over the whole range of values of x, whereas in (b) the scatter becomes greater, i.e. the residual deviations of y from the straight line increase in size as the rabbits get bigger.

Example 4

For $N = 10$, the 95 per cent confidence limit is 0.259, i.e. 25.9 per cent.

For $N = 100$, the 95 per cent limit is 0.030, i.e. 3.0 per cent.

Chapter 7

Example 1

(a) The expected numbers are 50 males and 50 females.

χ^2 (1 degree of freedom) $= (36 - 50)^2/50 + (64 - 50)^2/50 = 7.84$.

(b) $p = 0.64$ with 95 per cent confidence limits
$0.64 \pm 1.96 \sqrt{(0.64 \times 0.36)/100}$, i.e. 0.546 and 0.734. This sum is best done with fractions, not percentages, because the formula $p(1 - p)/N$ applies to fractions.
(c) The angular transform of 64 per cent is 53.1 degrees, with variance $820.7/100$. Its 5 per cent confidence limits are $53.1 \pm 1.96\sqrt{8.207}$, i.e. 47.5 and 58.7 degrees, corresponding to 54.3 and 73.0 per cent. The sum is done in percentages, because the angular transform is tabulated in percentages. In this example, the answers to (b), (c), and (d) are all very similar.

Example 2

Illustrates the 'tightness' of the scale of percentages near 100 per cent (Chap. 5). The answers to (b), (c), and (d) now differ; (c) and (d) make better sense than (b).

Chapter 8

Example 1

(a) Suppose there are N pigs per treatment. The standard error of the difference between two treatments will be $\sqrt{[0.0041(1/N + 1/N)]}$. If the

Answers

difference is 0·05 cm/per day and $t = 1·96$, then
$1·96 = 0·05/\sqrt{[0·0041(2/N)]}$, so that $N = 12·6$. There must be 13 pigs per treatment.
(b) *Either* proceed as in (a) *or*. the accuracy required is five times greater than in (a), therefore, the sample size must be twenty five times bigger, i.e. $N = 25 \times 12·6 = 315$.

Chapter 9

Example 1

(a) The mean square 1·773 is estimated from a sample of 244 values of y, and so has 243 degrees of freedom. The value 1·488 is a theoretical variance, and so has infinite degrees of freedom. The variance-ratio test is approximate, because it assumes the residuals $y - \bar{y}$ to be Normally distributed.
(b) The table of expected frequencies has six entries. There are two constraints imposed on those expected frequencies, namely the total must equal the sample size 244, and the mean of y must equal the observed value 1·488. Therefore, χ^2 has four degrees of freedom. The χ^2 test is approximate because it assumes the differences (observed − expected frequencies) to be Normally distributed.

Chapter 10

Example 1

The analysis of variance splits the total sum of squares into two or more parts which cannot be negative, whatever the data may be (Example 7, Chap. 2). It is only when we come to interpret the results of the analysis of variance, that we have to assume additive models and Normal distributions of remainders. Therefore, those assumptions are not part of the arithmetic method of analysis, but of the interpretation of the calculated mean squares. The genetic and environmental components of variance represent one way of interpreting the mean squares. They depend on the assumption of additivity in the model of eqn (10.1). If that model is seriously wrong, the analysis of variance itself is unaffected − in particular, the sums of squares cannot be negative − but the results cannot be interpreted in terms of an additive model, and therefore the components of variance, which are estimated from the mean squares in an attempt to interpret those mean squares, cannot be trusted, and may indeed be negative.

Chapter 13

Example 1

Using natural logarithms, the 'residual' mean square of log y in (a) is 0·2162 and in (b) is 0·0747. So formula (b) gives the better fit. Two formulae may be compared in this way, only when they are fitted by least squares to the *same* variate, in this case to log y. We cannot directly compare the accuracies of one formula fitted to y, and another fitted to (say) log y. But when the regression is linear, and we are regressing different transformations of y on the same x-variate, we can compare the correlations instead (Example 2(b)).

Example 2

Reasonable trial values for k in part (a), and for a in part (b), are determined by inspection of the original data, or by first trying a few widely spaced values. The analysis could be prolonged by taking a further fine range of values near $k = 0.0125$ and $a = 0.005$, but the improvement would hardly be worth the trouble. In (b), the y-variate itself changes as a changes, and so we cannot ask, 'Which value of a gives the smallest 'residual' mean square?', but ask instead, 'Which value of a gives the greatest correlation between y and t?' The regression equation is then $\log_e(100/N - 0.005) = 1.2827 - 0.0173t$, hence $N = 100/(0.005 + 3.60e^{-0.0173t})$. The value of a (0.005) is small compared with b (3.606). If it were zero, we should be back at the purely exponential growth curve used in Example 1 (Chap. 3)

INDEX